MARZIPAN AND MAGNOLIAS

MARZIPAN
AND
magnolias

ELIZABETH LANCASTER

Marzipan and Magnolias

First published in 2010 in Australia and New Zealand by Finch Publishing Pty Limited.

This edition published in 2020 by the author.
www.elizabethlancaster.com.au

Copyright © 2010 Elizabeth Lancaster

The author asserts her moral rights in this work throughout the world without waiver. All rights reserved. This eBook belongs to the author and, as such, no part of it may be copied, reproduced or transmitted by any person or entity (including Google, Amazon or similar organisations), in any form whatsoever (including via any electronic or mechanical means, including photocopying, recording or by any information storage or retrieval system) without the express prior written permission of the copyright holder.

The National Library of Australia Cataloguing-in-publication entry:

Author: Lancaster, Elizabeth.
Title: Marzipan and magnolias / Elizabeth Lancaster.
ISBN 9780648680260 (pbk.)
Subjects: Lancaster, Elizabeth.
Mothers and daughters – Australia – Biography.
Women – Australia – Biography.
Dewey Number (pbk): 306.8743092

Cover design by Michelle Miller
Internal design by Zena Shapter

Typeset in Caflisch Script Swash and Garamond.

Table of Contents

1. Venus – 1981	9
2. The Grapevine – 1967	13
3. Driving to Evans Head	19
4. Love and Language	31
5. Love and Language (ii)	43
6. Phone Calls	59
7. Café Kranzler	67
8. Phone Calls (ii)	77
9. The Taste of Marzipan	85
10. The Dress Looks Lovely	89
11. The Magnificent	99
12. The Piano	111
13. Caesar Salad	117
14. Snowstorm	125
15. Cape Cod	133
16. Twilight Zone	145
17. Marzipan (ii)	151
18. Idiots and Icons	157
19. A Send-off of Sorts	165
20. Downsizing	181
21. The Magnolia	187
22. The Casserole Committee	201
23. The Wedding Photo	207
24. French Polish	215
25. Sounds and Silence	225

To Mum

1. Venus – 1981

SOMETIMES I WONDER what happened to my first patient in the neurology ward of the inner-city Sydney hospital where I worked as a new graduate. She was about twenty-two and called herself Venus. Dyed black hair framed her ultra-white face, and safety pins dangled from one ear. Venus was of 'no fixed address'; she was tough and cool and she had multiple sclerosis.

Venus's boyfriend and only visitor was a male version of herself – safety pins and dyed black hair. He took her for walks, pushing the hospital wheelchair relentlessly up and down the corridor, the rhythmic squeak of the axle reporting their progress. Venus's hands lay in her lap, wrists taut and fingers kinked from spasticity. But her 'fuck-you' expression defied anybody to pity her.

She was my age, but with street cred. I felt like Miss Prissy in my prim white uniform, matching white shoes and a badge identifying me as an occupational therapy intern, a beginner. My supervisor sent me to interview her. 'Find out how she's managing,' she instructed me.

Venus wasn't going to make it easy for me.

'Cool earring,' I said.

She just looked at me. So did her boyfriend. I fumbled my words as I tried to find out how she managed at home, well, wherever it was she resided.

'I don't stop anywhere for more than a couple of days, *Elizabeth*,' she said, dragging out the syllables of my name. She made it sound so pompous, so staid.

My job was to ascertain a patient's level of independence in caring for themselves, and to what extent they were impeded by physical or cognitive deficits. Many went on to rehabilitation centres, but for others a home visit may have been necessary to install equipment, such as handrails in the bathroom or beside stairs. Venus, however, had no bathroom to call her own and despite her obvious mobility problems, was not interested in discussing the issue of stairs.

As I left the ward to return to my supervisor, I glanced into each of the six-bed rooms filled with patients displaying a confronting array of symptoms, the results of stroke or illness or head injury. Those who had undergone surgery bore an angry C-shaped wound on their shaved skulls, closed by thick staples – like a grotesque spoof on Zorro – a 'C' that stood for Craniotomy.

That morning I'd attended my first team meeting where the patients were discussed by doctors, nurses and therapists. The meeting was led by the senior registrar.

'Bed Nine to be discharged today. Beds Ten, Eleven and Twelve for theatre. Bed Fourteen's results came back positive.'

I wondered what it was like to be Bed Fourteen, receiving the news. There was no Bed Thirteen in this hospital because of thirteen's reputation as an unlucky number. Patients assigned to

Marzipan & Magnolias

Bed Fourteen were unaware of this administrative sleight of hand and so didn't think to blame their diagnosis on bad luck. But I knew the trick.

My supervisor was unsympathetic when I reported my failed efforts with Venus and told me to try again. But before I'd summoned the courage, I heard she had absconded in the squeaky wheelchair to marry the boyfriend. My enormous relief that I did not have to face her again would puzzle me for years to come.

2. The Grapevine – 1967

I WAS WOKEN by thumping coming from the direction of the kitchen – loud, almost aggressive. THUMP, THUMP, THUMP. I knew what it was: Mum wielding a heavy wooden mallet. She'd take it over her head and bring it down hard onto the stems of defenceless hydrangeas. Smashing the stalks to smithereens before placing them in water was good for them, according to Mum.

The sound was familiar enough. It was odd though, to be woken by it at seven o'clock in the morning in the middle of the school holidays.

'Quick, Libby, run out and pick a few more hydrangeas with big heads. There's a gap here I need to fill,' she called.

Although she couldn't see me, her sixth sense told her I was out of bed, awaiting her instruction. She never asked my brothers to pick hydrangeas for her; they wouldn't have had a clue. But, at seven years old, I knew what a hydrangea was, and a dimorphotheca and a cotoneaster. Almost by osmosis, I'd absorbed the information from Mum, like a child absorbing a second language from a foreign parent. I didn't mind being singled out to pick the flowers; from an early age I had the sense there was something special about being the only girl.

'Libby! The hydrangeas! I need to get this finished. And grab a few skeleton leaves if they look ready.'

For her dried arrangements, my mother prepared 'skeleton leaves'. She'd take stems of magnolia leaves, remove any foliage surplus to requirement, and with a Morticia Adams flourish, plunge them head-first into a bucket of water, where they spent six weeks decomposing. At precisely the right moment, they'd be retrieved, the leaves having been transformed into almost translucent geometric patterns of veins connected by a gossamer-thin film as sheer as the finest spider web.

By the time I returned to the kitchen, my two bleary-eyed brothers were out of bed.

'You're all going next door for the day,' Mum announced without looking up from her arrangement. Her tone did not invite further questioning and my brothers and I sat down to our Weet-Bix in silence. 'Libby, could you get Tim ready?'

I was four years older than the baby of the family (although his position as youngest would soon change with the birth of another brother, Matthew). I washed his face but before I could organise his clothes it was time to go. Mark, a grown-up eleven-year-old announced that he'd go over there when he was ready but Mum bundled us all out the door and marched us up the front path.

We knew our neighbours well. Both families had three children and there was much impromptu babysitting. Still, I don't ever recall being so unceremoniously deposited there as we were on this particular morning.

Mum knocked firmly on the front door – another departure from the norm. She usually just strolled in with a casual, 'It's only me,' to announce her arrival.

Elaine Jones, wrapped in a dressing gown, came to the door and gave us a welcoming, if surprised smile. My mother launched straight in.

'I need to leave the kids here for the day. They've had breakfast.'

Scanning our little group, Elaine's eyes settled on my younger brother. I cringed with embarrassment when I noticed the fossilised Weet-Bix on his tracksuit top.

'Okay, but we're having Brian's clients for dinner tonight, so I'll be busy. Is anything wrong?'

'No, I just have to go to town.'

Elaine looked perplexed but my mother had already turned on her high heels and was heading home. It was her high heels that were the oddest part of the morning so far. My mother never wore high heels, yet there they were on her feet, click-clacking up the path.

After she disappeared from view, an awkward silence hung in the air, but Elaine recovered quickly and took us inside.

When Mum returned that afternoon, she still had a strangely detached air about her. She scooted us out the door, but before she could follow, I heard Elaine stop her.

'Ruth, wait a moment. Something's wrong – what is it?'

'Dad died this morning,' said Mum, matter-of-factly. 'Thanks for having the kids.'

I don't remember being officially told of my grandfather's death.

He lived in Kyogle in northern New South Wales, so perhaps we would have remained none the wiser, had I not overheard that exchange.

It's not that my mother didn't love her father. In fact, he provided her with the guiding philosophies for life and his wisdom was quoted frequently throughout my childhood. 'Old Chester used to say...' and then Mum would fill in the blanks for whatever lesson was required.

'Old Chester used to say that all religions were stupid and were responsible for practically every war ever fought...' or, 'Old Chester used to say that funerals were evil things run by shallow men out to exploit your misery.'

We children had barely known Old Chester, seeing him only on his rare visits to Sydney, or when we made the annual drive to Kyogle, where Mum had grown up. So for me, his loss was more theoretical.

However, it did make me wonder about what it meant to be dead, the blackness of which, I imagined, must be infinite. I'd only recently learned about the concept of infinity. Space, apparently, was infinite. When I asked my father how it was possible that space went on forever, he told me to picture space being surrounded by a wall. That was easy enough to do.

'What's on the other side of the wall?' he asked.

'Nothing,' I said.

'Exactly. That's what space is.'

I entertained myself for long periods trying to grasp the enormity of it.

Death seemed to have something in common with space. Once

dead, a person is infinitely dead. They will never stop being dead. At least, that's the case if you don't complicate the scenario with religious beliefs and stories of an afterlife. Not that there was any danger of that happening in our family.

After my grandfather left this earth for an infinite future of being dead, I began to wonder about a funeral. My limited knowledge of funerals was based on TV images, where everything played out on a grand scale. Black cars, people in dark suits and a sombre atmosphere set the scene. But what did people *do* at a funeral? What was the *point?* I wanted to ask my mother about it, but after another overheard conversation, this time between her and her brother, Bruce, I decided not to raise it. My uncle was a mild-mannered, quietly spoken man, calm almost to a fault. I could not imagine his voice rising at the other end of the phone to meet the stridency of my mother's.

'No, I'm definitely *not* going,' she thundered into the mouthpiece.

A short pause for a response.

'I don't know – I'll pick grapes or something.'

Another short pause.

'If you want to waste all that money on a funeral, go ahead. But you'll be doing it without me. Old Chester used to say the only thing in this world that *shouldn't* be privatised is the bloody *crematorium*. People shouldn't be able to make money out of other people's suffering. It's an *evil* place and I won't be stepping foot into it.'

Several days later, after spending more time with the neighbours,

Elizabeth Lancaster

I came home to find the grapevine, which covered the pergola in our courtyard, practically stripped bare. I hadn't yet asked for an explanation about funerals, but I suspected the answer was somehow mysteriously linked to the current state of our grapevine.

3. Driving to Evans Head

AFTER MY GRANDFATHER DIED, we might never have gone to Kyogle again. Mum's home town held no sentimental allure for her at all. She found country towns claustrophobic and narrow-minded – everybody interfering in everybody else's business.

There was still one attraction, though. Her aunt lived there on a small dairy farm, which she ran almost single-handedly, despite an allergy to cows. Great Aunt Alice was the consummate gardener and her garden held a smorgasbord of botanical delights. Mum had inherited the gardening gene and would travel any distance for an exotic specimen, so every January, at the height of summer, we were loaded into the car and headed north.

Aunt Alice also owned a beach cottage at Evans Head, about thirty miles from the farm. This is where we spent most of the holiday. As much as I loved Evans Head, by the time I was fifteen I needed more than my brothers for company, so Mum suggested I bring a friend.

I took a chance and invited the glamorous new girl, Natasha, who had recently joined my school. All the girls had lined up to be Natasha's best friend, so it was a real coup when she accepted my offer.

Before the trip I warned her about the long drive: that we'd have to leave before dawn; that one of my brothers (Tim) got car sick; that the dog regularly 'broke wind' – as my mother delicately put it; and that this year we were also taking the duck.

Natasha arrived the night before with her things in a stylish little suitcase and matching carry bag.

'You'd better get a garbage bag for Natasha to put her things in,' Mum said.

Natasha looked to me for explanation. The reason for the trip, of course, was to stock up on Aunt Alice's plants. One year Mum had loaded so many plants in the boot that the luggage had to be sent back to Sydney by train. Since then, we'd packed our clothes in large green garbage bags so they could be squashed together, leaving more room for the plants.

I'd never questioned the garbage bag logic before, but now a small alarm bell rang in the back of my mind. Natasha handled it admirably, though, barely turning a hair as her neatly pressed belongings were upended into a No Frills plastic bag. After dinner, Dad went out to the garage to pack.

'Could everyone put their stuff near the front door?' he called out. 'And no argument about which car you're in.'

This year we were travelling in convoy – Dad in the Mazda and Mum in the Valiant. With the option of two vehicles, my youngest brother Matthew and I spotted an opportunity to be in a different car to the vomiting Tim. But before anyone could speak, Mum announced the seating arrangements.

'Libby, you girls and Tim should come with me, and bring the duck. Dad can take Matthew and Puff.' Puff was the obese and flatulent kelpie. She needed the back seat to herself, as she darted constantly from side to side to look out the windows.

'Why can't Dad take Tim, and Matthew can come with us?'

'You know that Tim feels sick when Puff breaks wind. We'll swap around at Bulahdelah when Tim's stomach has settled.'

Tim looked smug and I felt like slapping him, but I restrained myself in front of Natasha.

My brothers were excited about the long drive because they could use Dad's new CB radio, which he'd recently bought for work. As a real estate agent he was constantly driving between 'open houses' and the office to collect messages. A CB radio was an essential piece of technology for the up-to-date real estate agent. Not that Dad had thought of that. It was Tim who convinced Dad to get one. In a way, it was really Tim's CB radio set. It was even licensed to him. He'd been the one to decipher the instruction booklet and was now enjoying the opportunity to instruct us, in his usual didactic fashion, on the correct use of call signs. The fact that he did this with a lisp just made him all the more slappable.

'There'th a thpecial language you thpeak on a Thee Bee radio. For exthample, you don't thay "Where are you?" You thay "What'th your Ten-nine?" And you have thpethific call thignth to identify yourthelf.'

My eyes glazed over. I hated it when Tim told me anything, probably because he was younger than me and knew pretty much everything about everything. Sometimes he'd ask what I was studying in science. If I told him, he'd quiz me and correct my answers. I was totally unable to appreciate his gifted brain and would rather have failed science than have it explained to me by Tim.

'Why do we need call signs, anyway?' I asked irritably. 'We know who we are.'

'That'th jutht how it ith.'

As Natasha and I were preparing for bed, I tried to make light of my nerdy brother.

'You get used to Tim. At least he's not allowed to take his chemistry set – last year he made rotten egg gas and we had to stay out of the house for the whole day.'

But when I took my garbage bag out to be packed, I noticed Tim smuggling a suspiciously rectangular-shaped garbage bag into the boot that didn't look as if it contained t-shirts and shorts. I considered dobbing, but worried that would reflect badly on me.

'What about your older brother?' Natasha asked. 'Isn't he coming?'

'No, Mark says he's never going back to Evans Head. Oh, but don't worry – that's just him. He hates the outside toilet. I guess it does stink a bit. Mark once went for three weeks without using it, but Mum said he regretted it and had to eat prunes for weeks.' I wished that I could shut up. 'But it'll be great – once we get there.'

Next morning we set out before dawn in the following configuration: Mum led the forward contingent with Tim in the front seat and Natasha, me and the duck in the back. In the follow-up vehicle were Dad and Matthew in the front and Puff in the back.

The roar of our generously proportioned Valiant scared birds from their trees as Mum backed down the driveway, followed by Dad in the more modest Mazda. After one U-turn for Mum to check the iron was switched off, we were under way. Only the first rays of morning light were visible and we snuggled up with rugs in the cool pre-dawn air.

It didn't take long for the scene to change. Tim began devouring snacks at an alarming rate while I battled to hoard Natasha's and my share before it disappeared. I offered Natasha the last Space Food stick, but she declined, explaining that she rarely ate much before 5:30 in the morning. 'Me either,' I said, concealing the clutch of biscuits in my hand.

'Tim, why can't you take the duck for a while?' I demanded, trying to shift the focus from food. The duck, which had been a gift from our neighbour to Tim, was being relocated to Aunt Alice's farm. Mum was sick of its bad attitude at meal times and the way it used our swimming pool as a toilet. It was in a cardboard box for the trip, which was a tall order for a duck with attitude. In no time it had worked its beak out the top and it was taking swipes at anyone within reach. Before long its head and body followed and it strutted from one side of the car to the other, quacking demands for food. Attempts to replace it in its box were met with angry snaps of its beak.

The argument was interrupted by an unearthly sound from the front, as Tim lost the contents of his breakfast into an ice-cream bucket. This was routine for him, and I immediately stuck my head out the window. Natasha followed suit, but once again, the alarm bell sounded in my head.

'Aren't we going to stop?' Natasha asked weakly.

'It's too dangerous on the shoulder of the road,' said Mum. 'If a truck came along, we'd all be wiped out. Tim, call Dad on the CB and tell him we need to stop at the next garage.'

'Thee Q Thee Q November Alpha Yankee One-Three-Eight, come in,' said Tim, officiously.

There was a loud crackling sound like the rush of air, and then, 'Hello, hello?' It was Dad.

'No!' snapped Tim. 'You have to thay, thith ith November Alpha Yankee. Over.'

'Yes. Okay. We used to have to do this in signals in the air force.'

'Well thay it! Oh, forget it. Jutht put Matthew on. Over.'

'Hey there, Red Devil, this is Black Demon,' said Matthew.

'You know it'th illegal to uthe unlithenthed call thignth!'

'Yeah, well, what do you want?'

'We have to thtop at the nextht garage becauthe I've been thick. Over.'

Despite the pressing need for a pit-stop, our progress was as unhurried as ever. Mum never allowed Dad to speed or overtake (a constant source of muttering through gritted teeth from Dad) and Mum drove so slowly you could have picked things up off the road. Eventually, we pulled into a garage in Newcastle to fill up the car, wash the ice-cream container and have something to eat. Carsickness never affected Tim's appetite. He was ordering a chiko roll and chips when Mum's voice boomed across the cafeteria.

'Tim, what did you bring up back there?'

Natasha looked alarmed. 'Your mother can't be serious,' she whispered.

At first I was nonplussed. Then, as if seeing my family for the first time, I viewed the scene playing out before me. I saw the stunned looks on the faces of our fellow diners and, with a flash of insight, realised there were some things people just didn't say out loud. Tim didn't mind though, and provided a detailed response.

'Maybe we should wait outside,' I said. 'We should let the duck out for a run, anyway.'

Once we'd all eaten (except Natasha, who was off her food) we were on the road again. As promised, our seating positions were rearranged and we continued the journey thus: Dad and Tim in the front of the Mazda, with Natasha and me in the back, and Mum and Matthew in the front of the Valiant with Puff and the duck in the back.

'How come we have Tim again?' whispered Natasha, who had not recovered from the ice-cream bucket incident. It was a good point, which I raised with Mum over the radio.

'Because,' she said impatiently, 'perhaps if I have Puff in the back, the duck will stay in its box, but Tim can't travel with Puff. I've already explained that. Now, no more about it. We'll swap again next time we stop.'

The landscape gradually changed from forests to banana plantations to sugar cane country. These hours were filled with my brothers bickering across the airwaves over the legality of Matthew calling himself Black Demon. Periodically, Mum's voice came blasting through the speaker to warn Dad of an impending death trap on the road ahead and Dad muttered unintelligible responses. Natasha and I chatted easily enough, but I was preoccupied. The road-side cafeteria scene had been more disturbing than I cared to admit.

At least the worst of the trip seemed to be behind us. Tim's stomach had adapted to the car's movement and there would probably be no more meal stops. As we drove through the main street of Grafton, my thoughts were interrupted by Mum's urgent instruction, blasting through the CB radio:

'John, stop the car. I think I saw a cousin.'

I offered up a silent prayer. Even worse than Tim's carsickness would be for Mum to spot a relative. Perhaps it was because she came from a small family in a small town which she'd left many years before, but she went to great lengths to turn perfect strangers into blood relations. Usually, her modus operandi was to accidentally overhear a conversation in a café or a petrol station and establish a link. In the past we'd found ourselves invited back to our new relations' homes for tea and biscuits. Once we even got to stay the night when Mum found previously unknown kin in a town where our car had broken down.

'We stop at the only set of lights in town and you think you spot a cousin.' I could tell Dad was gritting his teeth.

'Look, there he is, coming out of that post office – the one with no legs.'

'I don't believe this.'

'Yes, he lost his legs in Changi. Stop the car. No, drive around the corner – you're in a Mazda.'

'What?'

'A Mazda. It's ... you know ... Japanese,' she had lowered her voice and we could barely make it out over the crackling airwaves.

Argument would be futile and Dad pulled into the kerb around the corner. Large veins were sticking out on his neck. It was a scorching day and the vinyl car seats were becoming intolerable. I imagined Natasha's eyes boring a hole into the side of my head, and suddenly it was all perfectly clear: my family was weird. I was left to contemplate this uncomfortable fact while Mum disappeared to find the legless cousin.

We all got out, animals included, and sat on the footpath in the shade of a Jacaranda tree. Nobody spoke. Even the duck seemed to have lost its edge. I wandered around the corner and from a safe distance, observed Mum doing her thing. She was gesticulating enthusiastically, pointing first to the north and then to the south. I tried to imagine the conversation. Wasn't he (the cousin – insert name) from up near Broadwater? She was Ruth Lancaster, originally from Kyogle, now from Sydney, blah, blah, blah. There appeared to be no response from her quarry and at last she sort of bowed (in apology?) and backed away.

So a case of mistaken identity that even my mother was unable to overcome allowed us to resume our journey. For the final leg, Matthew came in the Mazda with Natasha and me. Tim went with Mum, and they kept both animals, despite Tim's aversion to Puff's farts. I spent the remainder of the drive mentally checking off potential liabilities that could further condemn us.

The outdoor dunny was perhaps a bigger problem than I'd previously thought. If Dad parked the car at the back, as he always did, we'd have to walk right past it when we arrived. It was only emptied once a week, which in summer was a bit hard to take, but that wasn't really our fault. And surely no one could blame us for keeping old porcelain pots under the bed for night use. After all, maybe Mum was right about death adders hiding in the long grass between the cottage and the outhouse. It was true you wouldn't see a redback on the toilet seat in the dark. But what would Natasha think? She usually spent the summer at Palm Beach.

In the background, Matthew continued to needle Tim via the radio: 'Hey, this is Black Demon. Why are you lot driving so slowly?' etc, until he was interrupted by an angry third party.

'This is Black Demon here and you'd better stop using our call sign or you're dead meat.'

It took Matthew only a moment to recover his confidence and, emboldened by the anonymity of CB communication, he continued.

'What are you gonna do about it?'

'We're gonna pulverise you, you little smart-arse.'

'And how are you gonna find me?'

'We're right behind you. So pull over and let's see how tough you are.'

Matthew's head spun around on his shoulders as though it were spring-loaded, and he was met by the sight of a hotted-up Holden V8 right on our tail. He sank down low in his seat.

'How did you know it was us?' he squeaked.

'Hold on a moment,' interrupted Dad. 'I'm sure we can work this out.'

'Shut up, old man. If you don't pull over, we're gonna start ramming your rear-end.'

Dad pulled over, as did Mum a safe distance ahead of us. As

Dad got out of the car, he pulled on his white terry towelling hat, as if to fortify himself. Two loutish looking teenagers got out of the car behind. Matthew, Natasha and I barely breathed as we watched Dad approach the youths.

After lengthy negotiations, Dad somehow managed to appease them and swore that Matthew would never use their call sign again (something Tim would gloat about for years). The thugs roared off, leaving the smell of burning rubber in their wake.

'Wow,' said Natasha. 'Does that sort of thing happen often?'

'No, of course not,' I said, still shaking inside.

'Wow,' she said again. I wondered if I detected a note of excitement in her voice.

We finally arrived at Evans Head in the late afternoon, stiff as boards from the drive. Dad opened the boot to lug in a load of garbage bags. His thin, black hair was limp and sweaty and his glasses kept sliding down his nose. Within a few steps the cheap plastic bags exploded, spilling their contents onto the driveway, and I could hear Dad muttering through his clenched teeth.

My brothers had disappeared to the river with Puff and their fishing rods, leaving Natasha and me to help carry bursting garbage bags through the long grass and a cloud of flies hovering around the outhouse. Once again, I tried to explain the situation away.

'It's just because of the plants. If we didn't need to fit the plants in we'd use suitcases like everyone else.' But I felt it was a losing battle. What had I been thinking to invite her with my family for a whole month? I now looked at the cottage I loved so much with fresh eyes. Technically, it was more shack than cottage and I hadn't noticed before that the roof was rusty.

'Libby, don't worry – it's okay. I don't think your family needs suitcases. You're just not suitcase people.'

'*I'm* a suitcase person!' I cried. I had been unfairly tarred with the same brush as the rest of my family, but Natasha was already out of earshot. She had swung her garbage bag over her shoulder and was heading down to the shack, with the duck waddling happily behind her.

4. Love and Language

FROM THE AGE OF EIGHT I attended the same girls' school that Mum was sent to as a boarder in the 1940s. The uniform had barely changed in the intervening years and I loved looking through old memorabilia from Mum's time there. She had won prizes for piano performances and was a member of the Twelve Voice Choir in the soprano section. That choir still existed and was the most prestigious of musical ensembles. When I was old enough I tried out for it but only made it into the general choir as an alto. Compulsory chapel services gave me ample opportunity to sing with enthusiasm, hoping to be elevated one day to the premier choral group.

Even more impressive than Mum's musical endeavours was the fact that she was a boarder. To me the idea of moving away from your family seemed exciting and scary and part of me wished that I was a boarder.

Mum's parents had had to struggle to send her away to school. It was wartime and they were still suffering the effects of the Great Depression – not that they'd had much money before that, but afterwards things were really tight. So after paying the school fees, her father could only afford for her to come home once a year.

Mum would sometimes recount the story of that gruelling trip on the overnight mail train: fifteen hours, stopping at every station between Sydney and Kyogle for the guard to drop off the mailbags. She stood for the entire journey because Chester's finances didn't extend to the additional cost of a booked seat. But every leg-aching, foot-swelling minute was, apparently, worth it, to escape the confines and social pigeon-holing of Kyogle.

I could never understand Mum's disdain for the country. To me, those wide streets and charming two-storey corner pubs with wrought iron balconies, set against rolling green hills was surely a perfect existence. Even better than living in a country town would have been to live on a farm. I wouldn't have cared what type of farm, but for my mother, that had been the sticking point. To be a sheep or cattle grazier was one thing, but a dairy farmer was quite another. Her father was the latter: the lowest in the rural pecking order.

Chester had moved the family to town when Mum was five so she could attend school but he continued to work the dairy farm. Even at that age she was conscious of the social hierarchy.

'Sometimes, the teacher asked the children to stand up and tell the class what their fathers did for a living,' she would tell me. 'Mabel Black always wanted to go first.' Mum would put on her annoying parrot-like Mabel Black voice.

'My father's the Grave Digger.' She'd say it over and over. 'My father's the Grave Digger.'

'So?'

'Well, as a child I didn't think dairy farming required any

special skill or knowledge. Anyone could do it. At least Mabel's father had a *profession*,' she said. 'After digging the grave, he'd hot-foot it back to town and change into his mourning suit. Then he'd lead the funeral cortege on foot, with a sombre expression. All the men in town would gather on the footpath and remove their hats as the procession passed by.'

'I'd rather my father was a dairy farmer,' I said.

'Old Chester couldn't abide Mr Black. He used to say he didn't want Black leading his funeral procession through town.'

Mum's escape to Sydney as a thirteen-year-old had given her a chance to re-invent herself. A girls' boarding school, followed by Women's College and Sydney University put light years between her and her dairy farming roots.

While my mother was moving away from her past, I was embracing it. Her stories from boarding school days had made me wish I was from somewhere else – anywhere else. Having spent my entire life in the same suburb, same house, even the same school, I felt as bland as the apricot brick houses that surrounded me. I longed for an exotic story to tell. Mum's was the most interesting story I knew, so whenever possible, I'd drop into the conversation that she was from the country, as if by extension that made me more interesting, too.

Compared to my school friends, though, I couldn't compete. Many of them had parents or grandparents from *overseas*. My nearest foreign relative was my great-great-great-something-grandfather who was transported to the colony in 1788 for stealing a bolt of fabric. I felt that I carried the cumulative burden of two hundred years of banishment to the end of the earth, where I was now trapped.

During my primary school years, television provided a window of sorts onto the rest of the world. Although most of the offerings of the sixties left me bored and restless there was one show that had me hooked: *I Love Lucy*. While Lucy's foolish exploits frustrated me, Desi Arnaz and his South American accent and word muddles were irresistible. In one episode he accused Lucy of 'yelling tiger' after she'd feigned crisis once too often. My brother, Mark, had to explain the 'crying wolf' reference, but once I got it, it was official: I was in love with Desi Arnaz. Was it the way he spoke, or was it also his Latin temperament? If only I were Latin. I'd dress up in my mother's lacy blue wedding dress, by then full of holes and kept in our dress-up box. Rattling a couple of seed pods from a jacaranda tree as castanets, and wearing a sultry look, I'd while away the afternoons imagining a different life with Desi.

I became preoccupied with foreign accents. Perhaps my father had the same preoccupation because I'd often hear him taking off someone's accent. Chinese, Italian, Hungarian, he could do them all. Dad hated receiving work phone calls at night, so if Mum called out to him that a Mr Wong or Mrs Ludiwici was on the line, Dad would be imitating their accent through clenched jaws as he reached for the receiver. 'Shut up, John,' my mother would hiss, covering the mouthpiece with her hand. 'They'll hear you.' My brothers would be laughing and egging him on, but I just wanted to know how he did it.

Marzipan & Magnolias

After leaving school, I spent three more bland years at college, but after graduating as an occupational therapist, I managed to land a job at St Vincent's Hospital in Sydney's inner city. Walking from Kings Cross Station to work each day, I'd pick my way around used needles, broken bottles and the odd person sleeping off the excesses of the night before. Ambulances and police cars roared up and down Victoria Street. I was finally close to some action.

The next step was to move out of home, which I did with Natasha (who'd stuck around despite the trip to Evans Head) and another girlfriend, Meredith. We three girls shoe-horned our way into a two-bedroom flat (Meredith volunteered to sleep on the enclosed verandah) a stone's throw from the ferry wharf in Neutral Bay.

At work, I was thrilled to be assigned to a ward with a nurse possessed of a full-blown Northern Irish accent and the captivating name of Moira McAffery. Moira's voice boomed across the ward every morning: 'Now, young man, I'll not be putt'n up with your shenanigans, on this fine mornin'.'

There was something totally compelling about Moira. I'd practise at home to get the vowel sounds right, but it was more than just how she put sounds together; it was a whole way of being Irish. Sometimes she brought in photos of young nieces and nephews still in Ireland. I'd search the photos for early signs of their Irishness, envying these toddlers who, no doubt, spoke like Moira without even trying.

At the height of my infatuation with this accent I met an Irishman named Seamus O'Malley. It was a blind date; he needed someone to take on a harbour cruise for a work function and a mutual friend, aware of my fascination with this accent, suggested me. I don't remember much about the cruise. I don't remember meeting anyone or eating anything. All I remember is sitting on the deck in the moonlight listening to the most beautiful accent I had ever heard.

We began seeing each other on a regular basis. Well, semi-regular, which meant when he made himself available. But I was happy to wait around. He was from the south and spoke in a soft, lilting melody about Ireland's troubled and romantic history: the centuries of suppression endured under British rule; the secrecy with which stories of resistance were passed from one generation to the next; and of the selfless patriots who had formed the Irish Republican Army. He spoke of Ireland with an ache that was almost palpable. I felt so unworldly with my suburban upbringing of fenced backyards and afternoon television (my introduction to multiculturalism notwithstanding). To add to the attraction, he was Catholic and I was Protestant, something he always teased me about.

'They'd torture a man by shooting him behind the kneecap to get information,' he said one evening, almost in a whisper.

'Who would do such a thing?'

'The Protestants, of course, Libby.' And then he'd laugh.

I fell for him big time. But it turned out to be a case of unrequited love. His only true passion was Ireland and he became melancholy every time he spoke of it. Many nights I stayed in, waiting for the phone to ring, and then accepted the ludicrous stories he'd come up with to explain his absences and rumours of other women.

My mother didn't like the sound of Seamus at all.

'He looks like a bus conductor,' she pronounced after her one and only brief meeting with him. 'Bog Irish.'

Such harsh criticism, even by my mother's standards, had no impact on me whatsoever. Meredith and Natasha, however, had more influence and begged me to get rid of him. I knew they were right but just as I'd resolve to end it, he'd win me back. I'd sit on his back porch while he played mournful Irish ballads on his guitar and sang with a voice so hauntingly beautiful it made the hairs on the back of my neck stand up. Then I'd be hooked again, until his next disappearing act.

Eventually, a strong sense of self-preservation forced me to end it, but my fascination with all things Irish continued. St Vincent's Hospital had many homeless people in its environs. Among them were a number of Irish, who were sometimes admitted after a fight or a fall. When I asked them about Ireland, they'd be overcome with the same melancholy that had afflicted Seamus, and a tear might even escape and roll down one cheek. Then I'd casually ask if they'd ever been married. Immediately a glint would appear in their eye and they'd say, as if describing a miraculous escape, 'Almost. A woman almost got me up the aisle once.'

This rudimentary social research revealed to me two important facets of the Irishman's psyche. The first: that although they chose to leave their homeland in droves, they were perennially, even pathologically homesick; and the second: that they considered the matrimonial noose a much graver fate than living on the streets.

After breaking it off with Seamus it was some months until my next close encounter with a foreign accent. It was owned by a German backpacker called Martin, whom I met through, of all people, my mother. The connection was via a maze so complex, dating back to her boarding school days, that it defies explanation. Suffice it to say that Martin arrived on her doorstep one day with the friend of a distant relative.

Although Mum had never met them, she invited them in for a cup of tea. She was so charmed by Martin's accent and European ways that, in a fit of extravagance, she announced that if he needed work, her daughter could help him find a job in a pub. She took his number, promising I'd get back to him.

'Mum, how would I get him a job in a pub?' I said irritably when she told me. Despite my curiosity, I had my pride. I didn't want an encounter arranged by my mother.

'You must know *someone* who could get him a job,' she said. 'He was charming – he had one of those lovely sports jackets with leather patches on the elbows. Anyway, he'd be a good contact for you to have when you travel. At least give him a ring.'

She handed me his number, which I shoved in my pocket, determined to overcome the temptation to call him.

As it happened, Martin rang me a few days later. He did, indeed, have a lovely accent, gentle and difficult to place. I explained that my mother had exaggerated my ability to help him find work in a pub, but he suggested we get together for a drink anyway.

St Vincents Hospital was just a short bus ride away from the Lord Dudley Hotel in Paddington so we arranged to meet there after I finished work the next day. I had to admit I was curious. I can't remember what method we used to identify each other but somehow we did. Martin was slim, fair and a little taller than me. He had an open, friendly expression that put me immediately at ease.

'Can I get you a drink?' he asked. 'I invite you.'

An interesting turn of phrase, I thought. He ordered a beer for himself and a Bacardi and coke for me, and we settled into a booth beside a window. Despite the pretext for our meeting, it quickly became apparent that the last thing Martin needed was my help in finding a job. He had just spent several months on a sheep station in Goodooga in north-western New South Wales, where he had learned to swear like an Australian bushman.

'I met this guy on a ferry in Hamburg,' said Martin. 'He was very nice and invited me to visit him on his bloody farm any bloody time. So I did.'

Now back in Sydney, Martin had more work than he could manage. His first job was as a travelling wine salesman, flogging French wine door to door. But without a car it was a hard slog lugging a box of wine around on the train. He then got work in a dry-cleaning business, which he juggled with yet another job at a Whale Car Wash. He was told he had a great future in both. To supplement his income he worked as a night auditor for a hotel in Kings Cross.

'I don't think you need any more work,' I said.

'That's true,' he said. 'But in these jobs I am feeling a bit like a frog out of water. Perhaps pub work would be better and I could meet more proper Aussies,' (pronounced with a strong 's'). 'Anyway, bugger it. Let's just celebrate.'

'Celebrate what?'

'You know – have another drink. We call it "celebrating" in Germany.'

The more he celebrated the more I enjoyed listening to him.

'I love your Sydney Harbour, but sailing here is not easy,' he said. 'I borrowed a laser for a competition on the weekend but the comedy boat kept yelling out to me to be disqualified.'

'The what boat?'

'The comedy boat. Bloody fuckin' hell. They just got in everyone's way, yelling out with their megaphones all their stupid rules. Finally, I had to pull out.'

'You mean the *committee* boat?'

'Yes. The comedy boat. Bloody bastards.'

A few days later, Martin called me again, this time to invite me to his impromptu farewell party. His trip had been cut short because his father was unwell and he needed to return home. I thought I should go as I didn't think he would have known many people in Sydney. I was wrong. Unbeknownst to me, he'd been sharing an apartment with Peter, an eccentric artist from the country, now living in Double Bay. This apartment was bursting with hip Sydney-siders including a glamorous blonde called Georgiana, who appeared to be fused to his left arm. Martin was the toast of the moment and I felt completely out of my depth (or perhaps like a frog out of water). I stayed for the obligatory hour or so and then made my excuses to leave.

He managed to detach himself from the blonde and ushered me towards the front door.

'You have told me that you will come to Europe one day,' he

said. 'Here is my address in Hamburg. Come and visit me.' His voice was soothing.

He walked me to my car. Then there was the moment, just like in the movies, where we looked at each other. We just looked. No kiss, no more words. Just a look, frozen in time. That was weird, I thought, as I drove away.

I was now twenty-two and without any prospective romantic liaison with an accent. Instead I had an overwhelming desire to get myself to Europe and immerse myself in – what exactly, I wasn't sure. I just had to get there. It took another year for me to save enough money for a one-way ticket.

About two weeks before I left, a letter arrived unexpectedly from Martin with a new address in Frankfurt, having apparently moved from Hamburg. *I remember you said that one day you would travel to Europe. Please come and knock on my door.* The words sent tingles through my fingers. Apart from a postcard he'd sent shortly after he left, this was the first I'd heard from him in over a year. I replied immediately, explaining that my departure was imminent and asking him to send his phone number to my parents who could forward it to me.

Several days before I flew out, Dad rang me at work.

'Libby, a telegram has arrived addressed to you. Should I open it?'

'Yes, please.' I'd never seen a telegram before, much less received one, and I couldn't imagine who would be sending one to me.

'It's from that Martin chap, you know, the German or Austrian who was here a few years ago. It says he's moved to Frankfurt and gives his address and phone number. Then it says, *"Have a 6000 trip".*'

'A what?'

'A 6000 trip. It's written in numerals. A six followed by three noughts. What does that mean?'

'I have no idea.'

I called in to my parents after work to inspect the message. I'd only ever seen telegrams in the movies before. Mum waved it in the air with a suspicious look on her face.

'What?' I said.

'If you stay in Germany I won't be sending the Duchess over to you.'

The Duchess was the antique dressing table my grandmother had given me for my twenty-first birthday. It was my most prized possession but lived at my parents' house because it was too big for the flat.

'I'm not planning to stay in Germany. Could I see the telegram, please?'

She was still waving it in the air. I plucked it out of her hand. Have a 6000 trip. What did it mean? I stuffed it in my pocket.

'I'm serious,' she said. 'I'm not sending the Duchess.' She smiled, but there was a note of warning in her voice.

5. Love and Language (ii)

AS A YOUNG WOMAN, Mum had had her own overseas adventure. After university, she and several of her friends from Women's College 'sailed' for England. As a small child I had imagined the ship to be something akin to Captain Cook's *Endeavour*, but I later learned it was a large cruise liner, on which it was usual for people to have 'shipboard romances'. Not Mum, though, because my father was left waiting for her in Sydney and they planned to marry on her return.

When I was preparing for my trip Mum pulled out her old photos of various iconic locations she had visited. She looked the same in every shot: 1950s sensible, short brown hair and a broad smile. There was one of her sitting on a camel in Cairo, the pyramids forming a backdrop to the picture. I couldn't imagine anything more exotic than riding a camel in Egypt. But I couldn't detect what she was thinking. She looked the same as in all the other photos: same hair, same smile. I couldn't put my finger on what was missing. She was there but not really *there*, as though she was one step removed from the situation. I asked her about riding the camel.

'Yes, his name was Moses and Bev's was called Canasta. I was wearing my pretty pink and green sandals. We didn't wear pants in those days and we'd dressed up to leave the ship for the day.'

I had the sense that what she loved most was the camaraderie with her girlfriends, and that without their presence the experience might not have existed at all. Everything was viewed through the lens of the group: she existed because the group existed. It was a point of difference between us. During school, I had also formed close friendships but I didn't have to be with my friends all the time. While Mum seemed to fully understand my desire to go overseas – part of an Australian's rite of passage – she wasn't sure why I would consider going alone. Even so, she took me shopping and bought me a shoulder bag, a backpack and a thermal sleeping bag. She told me how much she'd miss me, how lucky she was to have a daughter, and I knew she meant it. That was before the telegram from Martin had arrived.

The departure gates at Sydney's Kingsford Smith Airport had long occupied a special place in my imagination. Now, aged 23, I was finally going to find out what was on the other side. My parents, brothers and friends had all come out for the farewell. Dad bought everyone a drink in the bar but I was too excited to touch mine. After a quick sweep around the group to say goodbye, barely pausing to hear Mum's final instructions – something about keeping my passport strapped to my body – I watched myself disappear through those gates.

Thirty hours later, I arrived in Dublin. (My first stop was Ireland, just to see what all the fuss was about.) At last I could immerse myself in accents, and to my great satisfaction I too now had an accent.

I stayed with a friend from home who was studying medicine at Trinity College, and lived in a share house with other students. On my first morning I woke with a fright when someone walked into the lounge room where I was curled up on the couch.

'Oh, sorry. Who are you?' said an unidentified male voice.

It took only a moment for the fog of jetlag to lift.

'I'm a friend of Jamie's,' I said.

'Of course. You're the Australian, aren't you?'

A little shiver ran up my spine. Yes, I was the Australian. No name or details required. I crawled out of my sleeping bag and went to the window. It was early March and the faint blue sky seemed far away. The streetscape was so different from anything back home; two-storey white stucco houses with grey slate roofs and chimneys puffing smoke, all identical and lined up beside each other close to the street. It looked just as it was supposed to look. Once again, I felt that shiver.

My senses were sharpened to a new intensity. I perceived everything in superlatives: Dublin University was so phenomenally old, the town centre so adorably quaint, the hills so green and misty and the dry stone walls on the roadside, well, just so Irish. And the people were so Irish as well. They all spoke like Seamus and referred to each other as 'your man' or 'your woman'. In the evening I'd join Jamie and his friends at the pub. 'Aren't you going to introduce me to your woman?' they'd say to him. At first I thought they'd mistaken me for Jamie's girlfriend, but it was just their Irish way of chatting.

On my last night, one of the people I met was a medical student called Michael. From his accent I assumed he was Irish, so I was surprised to learn he was actually Dutch. In a matter of only a few years, he had acquired not only flawless English, but an authentic Irish accent as well. When the pub closed, Michael invited a small group of us back to his apartment. We all drank, although not to excess, and talked and laughed until dawn was breaking. Then in a panic, everyone scattered, realising they had just lost an entire night's sleep. Michael said I should make the most of my last day in Ireland, and offered to take me sightseeing to the Wicklow Mountains, just south of Dublin. Having been up all night, unsurprisingly, dense fatigue soon descended upon both of us. Michael said something I did not comprehend at all.

'What was that?' I asked.

He repeated the sentence but it still made no sense. I just looked at him, blankly. It was only then I realised he'd spoken in Dutch. He laughed, then resumed in English without missing a beat. But I was a beat behind. So far, I'd only met the Irish version of Michael. The idea of being able to slip between identities was captivating. How I *wished* I spoke another language.

It was dusk when I reluctantly boarded the ferry that crossed the Irish Sea to Holyhead in Wales. From the deck I watched the lights of Dublin fade, then disappear. My mind was so full I feared that everything after this would seem dull by comparison. Eventually, forced inside by the freezing wind, I checked out the cabin. There were several vacant seats, which I stretched across. Having not slept in forty-eight hours, I fell instantly into a dreamless sleep.

Marzipan & Magnolias

At that very deepest point of unconsciousness, I was jolted awake by the sound of a blaring foghorn. I jumped up, completely disoriented. Looking around stupidly, I tried to figure out my surroundings. The ferry, of course. I had to get off. I raced into the bathroom and was shocked by my reflection: puffy-eyed, and wild-haired, I looked slightly mad. I splashed water over my face, grabbed my backpack and charged out onto the deck. By now, properly awake, I joined the queue to disembark, hoping no one had witnessed my manic performance.

The next leg of the journey would be an overnight bus trip to London. As I waited, shivering on a seat in the bus shelter, a young woman, about my age, sat down beside me. She pulled a loaf of rustic-looking bread from her backpack and unwrapped some cheese to go with it. She offered me some.

'It's soda bread,' she said.

I'd never heard of soda bread but by now I was famished. We chatted for a while and I learned she was Swedish (she also sounded Swedish, so no confusion there). By the time we boarded the bus, I was so cold that I crawled into my sleeping bag, and still sitting bolt upright, fell instantly into another comatose sleep.

When I was next dragged to consciousness, it was broad daylight, and to my horror, the bus was filled with briefcase-wielding business people, gingerly stepping over my sleeping-bagged legs which were blocking the aisle. And again, I could make no sense of my surroundings. My overnight coach had transformed itself into a rush-hour bus. Trapped in my cocoon, I wriggled closer to the window. There was no sign of the Swedish girl or any of the other passengers from Holyhead. I felt utterly ridiculous.

Finally the bus arrived at Victoria Station and everybody piled out. I smoothed down my rumpled shirt and pushed my hair back from my face. Then with as much dignity as I could muster I hoisted my backpack over one shoulder and stepped out into the morning sunlight.

When I left Australia, for some reason I'd been determined to look like a seasoned traveller. So far, I was definitely not pulling that off. If I couldn't even get myself from Dublin to London without looking like a complete hobo, what hope did I have?

These thoughts evaporated, though, as I took in my surroundings: red double-decker buses, London cabs and businessmen in pin striped suits bustling to and fro. I could scarcely believe that it was really me standing in their midst. I felt like an extra in a musical, and almost wanted to burst into song.

There wouldn't be time to immerse myself in the experience yet, though, as I was booked on a bus-camping trip, departing the next morning. So the priority was to find to a laundromat, have something to eat and try to get a full night's sleep in a hotel.

The reason for choosing a camping tour as a way to see Europe was based on cost, however, the reality was that camping wasn't my thing. And there was a disappointing lack of diversity as many of us were Australian. There were a few from the US, a few kiwis and one couple from South Africa. All were great fun but the thrill I'd experienced in Ireland of being an outsider looking in was missing. By far the worst part about it was the pace. We rushed through cities and countries, pausing briefly at the various sights, only to pile back on the bus again. The tour guide droned on about local culture and history but we were not experiencing it. After a month of this cattle-herding approach to travel I began to go crazy. Unable to focus on the guide's endless travelogue, I found myself instead contemplating the words of Martin's mysterious telegram.

When my group arrived in Germany, I plucked up the courage to ring him. He sounded pleased to hear from me and suggested I visit right away.

'Why don't you leave the stupid tour?' he said. 'I have holidays owing. I can better show you Europe.'

In a rash decision, I agreed. I abandoned the tour and bought a train ticket from Heidelberg to Frankfurt, but even as I boarded I was having second thoughts. How many holidays exactly did he have owing? Were we talking a week or three months? But the thought of a comfortable bed, or at least a sofa and a hot shower that didn't require a constant input of coins, was so tempting I managed to overlook my concerns. And there was that small but undeniable thrill of anticipation.

As my train pulled into Frankfurt's *Hauptbahnhof* I wondered if I'd still recognise him or if he'd recognise me. The platform was packed with people and they all looked the same. How embarrassing it would be if I just walked right past him.

I got off the train with my backpack and stood for a moment. Announcements were blaring out from loudspeakers as people moved purposefully towards the exit. After a few minutes, the platform was practically empty. I hoisted my pack over my shoulders and began walking. There was someone walking towards me. That had to be him. Was it him? I squinted. From this distance he looked like so many other Germans. Fair hair, slim build. But unlike his compatriots, he walked with a distinct bounce to his gait, and as he drew closer, I detected a sort of openness about his expression that now seemed familiar. He strode over to me.

'So there is an Aussie koala on this big station, after all. Hello.' He kissed me on the cheek and took my backpack. Outside he hailed a taxi. He didn't have a car, he explained, as he could ride a bicycle to work, which he kept in the basement of his apartment. *His* apartment? There was no mention of anybody else – no flatmates or friends that he shared with. It had never occurred to me that he might live alone. This was suddenly sounding far too intimate. In Sydney, all my friends lived in share houses; I couldn't think of anyone my age who lived alone. The taxi dropped us outside an apartment block and we went up to the first floor. He unlocked the door and indicated for me to enter first. It was a one-room studio apartment with a tiny kitchenette off to the left. The entire main room seemed to be taken up by an enormous bed. I was such an idiot! Why hadn't I checked this out?

'I'll be sleeping on the floor,' he said. 'You have earned some comfort after having only a tent for so long.'

I was completely flummoxed. 'I don't mind the floor,' I blurted out. 'After all, I'm used to it.'

'I need to go and buy some things,' he said. 'In the refrigerator I have only some margarine and marmalade' (pronounced *marmalahda*). He opened the little bar fridge to illustrate his point. 'You can have a shower if you like and maybe I can show you the sights of Frankfurt this afternoon.'

From the window I watched him leave, heading, I presumed, toward the shops. I flopped onto the bed and thought about home for the first time in weeks. I realised that nobody had any idea where I was. Not a clue. I felt such a very long way away. I lifted my pack onto the bed and rummaged around for some clean clothes. At least I could have a hot shower.

That afternoon Martin did indeed show me the sights of Frankfurt: the town square, the old shopping and restaurant district, and the River Main. His time working on an outback sheep station in Australia was still evident and his use of the local expletives as conversation fillers sounded even more out of place here than it had in Sydney.

'Bloody fuckin' hell,' he'd say, without the slightest provocation.

'People don't usually say that in everyday conversation,' I said, almost sorry to enlighten him.

'They do in Goodooga,' he said. 'In Goodooga, that *was* the bloody conversation.'

He had bought various breads and cheeses and a bottle of red wine and suggested we have a picnic by the river. I'd never been keen on red wine but I didn't want to admit it – it just seemed so European to have red wine and cheese on a summer's afternoon by the river. The day had been warm so we chose a spot in the shade on the grassy bank. Martin spread out a rug and the food but noticed he had forgotten to bring a corkscrew for the wine. After a few Aussie expletives, he proceeded to try to force the cork down into the bottle by pressing on it with his thumb. As he pressed on the cork, we chatted about this and that. He told me he worked for the Intercontinental Hotel group, which allowed him free accommodation in cities around Europe.

'Would you like to go to France, or perhaps Italy?' he said. 'I can promise you the Intercontinental will be more comfortable than your tent.'

I wasn't sure what to commit to. I watched the cork progressing down the neck of the bottle, millimetres at a time, accompanied by a sort of squeaking sound.

'How long do you have off work?' I asked.

'Four weeks.'

With a final squeak the cork plopped into the bottle and bobbed up and down in the dark liquid.

'There,' he said, and poured me a glass.

Despite my previous indifference to red wine, it slid down very easily. Before long I felt as if I were in a movie – perhaps *The Sound of Music* meets *Roman Holiday*. He topped up my wine.

'I have to ask you,' I said, changing the subject from holiday plans, 'what did you mean by "Have a 6000 trip" in your telegram?'

'Have a what trip?'

'Six thousand, written in numbers, like this.' I took a pen from my bag and wrote the number on the paper wrapping of the cheese. He studied it for a moment, then laughed.

'Those bloody idiots at the post office. That is meant to say "GOOD". "Have a *GOOD* trip". They probably didn't understand English there.'

He took my pen and wrote 'GOOD' in capitals. All the letters were big and round, and lacked definition; I could see how someone could read it as 6000. I thought it best not to consider this fact for too long: that the mystery of the telegram came down to a case of poor penmanship. I took another sip of wine. It was a beautiful afternoon. Dappled sunlight peeked between the leaves of a grand elm tree and the River Main flowed lazily towards its destination. Martin leaned towards me and put one arm around my shoulders. He looked into my eyes, his gaze steady. I've often been told that when I look at people, I maintain an excessive amount of eye contact – enough to make them feel uncomfortable. A work colleague once told me that she thought I must either be very honest or a psychopath. Martin, it seemed, suffered from the same affliction. He was either going to have to kiss me, kill me or avert his gaze. He chose the former. His kiss was slow and gentle, like the flow of the river, and together we melted onto the soft grass of the riverbank.

'You have very sensible lips,' he whispered, and my heart gave a little leap.

We spent four romantic weeks together in France, staying at various Intercontinental Hotels. As a courtesy to Martin as a foreign colleague, we were always welcomed with a fruit basket or chocolates and champagne in our room. Having most recently slept in a tent, sometimes in the rain, it was heady stuff for me. And, of course, there was Martin's accent, smoothing the way, slipping seamlessly between German, French and English. He only spoke English to me, of course, so this was the persona I knew best. But when he accidentally caught his finger in the door one morning and yelled, '*Scheisse*!', I was taken aback. It had come straight from the heart, his German heart. That was his default language in an emergency. I experienced that same consternation as I had when Michael had spoken Dutch to me by mistake. I wondered again about the link between language and identity.

Martin and I spent our days between cafés, lying on a Mediterranean beach or sightseeing. We didn't talk about what would happen at the end of the holiday until we were back in Frankfurt and I was preparing to return to London where I could work and replenish my funds.

One morning while he was out, the phone rang. I wasn't sure whether to answer it or not, but the insistent beeps urged me to pick up. To my great surprise the voice at the other end was female and Australian. She sounded as shocked as I felt.

'Er, I'm a friend of Martin's. She pronounced his name with a stilted attempt at a European accent. 'Is he there?'

'No,' I said, deliberately evasive. 'Could I take a message?'

'It's Georgiana. Martin suggested I visit when I'm in Germany. I wanted to organise a time.'

'I'll tell him,' I said. My heart was thumping in my chest. After replacing the receiver, I sat motionless, staring ahead of me. I suddenly felt very foolish.

When Martin arrived home he was in an upbeat mood.

'I've checked with a travel agent,' he said. 'The airfares in Europe are cheap, so we can visit each other often. Or even better – you could just stay here with me until Christmas.'

'That might interrupt your next visitor from Australia,' I said with more sarcasm than I had intended.

He looked confused.

'Your friend Georgiana rang earlier. She said you'd invited her to come and visit. She'd like to know when.'

It took him a moment to register. Finally he said, somewhat weakly, 'I was just being polite.'

I began throwing things into my backpack, acutely aware that I was making a fool of myself. He must have thought I was an idiot. He probably had a constant parade of Australians passing through. What was I expecting?

'Elizabett.' (He never pronounced the 'th' at the end of my name.) He held my shoulders and turned me to face him. 'She's just a friend.'

But I no longer trusted my ability to make decisions about men, particularly foreign men. I should have learned that lesson a long time ago. Anyway, after four months of living out of a backpack I suddenly had an urge to slot into a normal nine-to-five routine and take stock. Despite Martin's protestations, I stuck to my guns.

So once again I found myself at Frankfurt's *Hauptbahnhof*.

'Please let me know where you're living and your phone number,' he said. 'I will visit you.'

He lifted my backpack onto the train and I went in to find a seat. I watched him through the window as we pulled out of the station. 'Call me,' he mouthed, and then he was gone.

I felt strange, numb, but as I settled into the comfortable clickety-clack of the train, my determination strengthened. There was still so much out there to experience.

Once back in London, I found share accommodation in a flat a stone's throw from Hyde Park, and took a three-month locum at the Central Middlesex Hospital. Red double-decker buses beetled along Bayswater Road at the end of my street, and the West End and Knightsbridge were just a quick tube ride away. It was just as exhilarating as when I'd first stepped off the bus at Victoria Station before my camping trip.

My flatmate was an Irish occupational therapist called Sinead. She was also new to London, was suspicious of the English, yet keen to meet a man. I was a handy side-kick to take to the pub where she hoped to find Mr Right. Her quest was in vain, but it meant we spent a lot of time together. When not musing on her elusive perfect match, Sinead chose to inform me on matters of faith. She found my dearth of knowledge and lack of conviction worrying. Initially, her sheer force of personality was compelling and it was curious to live in such close proximity to a real believer. However, her didactic ways wore thin and I set about establishing my own social life.

Despite my resolve to move on from Martin, I thought it would be churlish not to, at least, let him know my phone number – after all, we'd had a terrific time. The flat had a phone that allowed us to receive calls, but not make them, so I collected my coins and, feeling inexplicably nervous, walked to a phone box on the corner that smelled of cigarettes and urine. When he answered he sounded excited to hear from me, but I was determined to keep the conversation general.

'What are you doing tonight?' I asked him.

'I'm knitting,' he said in his gentle European accent that made me feel weak at the knees. He had somehow avoided the harshness many Germans have when speaking English.

'You can knit?'

'Well, somebody has to put the buttons back on my shirt.'

I felt my willpower slipping.

We continued our phone calls and he finally convinced me to fly to Frankfurt for a weekend. On the way to his apartment from the airport, it became clear he'd had a bad day. He went through all the things that had gone wrong, then, with a sweep of his hand he said sadly, 'It was hilarious.' My heart swelled.

At the airport on the Sunday night he said he wanted to apply for a transfer to London. Despite my misgivings about where this was heading, I agreed. I'd be able to test if there were more to this relationship than accents and grammatical errors; more than just 'yelling tiger'. However, obtaining a transfer to London turned out to be more difficult than he had anticipated ('So many bastards want transfers'). After some frustrating months and many calls from my stinking telephone box, he suggested, instead, that I go to Germany for Christmas.

Apart from that one weekend, I hadn't seen him for almost five months and was feeling apprehensive. As I emerged through the arrival gate at Frankfurt Airport, he strode up to me with such confidence and said simply, 'I bloody think I love you.' He looked straight into my eyes, waiting for my response. There was, of course, only one thing to say.

'I bloody think I love you, too.'

6. Phone Calls

AFTER RETURNING TO LONDON I learned that my temporary position working on the neurology ward had been extended for another few months. It was very similar to the job I'd left in Sydney, including the daily format beginning with a ward round. The 'team', which was organised into the same strict hierarchical structure, trailed the doctors from one bed to the next and listened in silence as pronouncements were issued on prognosis or plans for surgery. Monday mornings were often the busiest after weekend admissions of young people, following horrendous car or motorbike accidents. It was sometimes difficult to meet the gaze of families, still full of hope.

When I was not at work, the neurology unit might as well have been in another galaxy. It was as though I occupied two separate dimensions. There was my work and there was my life. The human dramas that unfolded each day between nine and five were contained and separate, like a soap opera on television that could be switched off; the characters held in suspended animation until I arrived again the next day.

It was curious to find myself on the other side of the world, confronted by the same array of frightened faces and assortment of peculiar symptoms that I'd seen in Sydney. I wondered about the never-ending supply of patients filling neurology wards around the world – people hapless or careless enough to fall victim to illness or disease – until I realised neurology wards would always be full. That's just the way things were.

As the winter months in London dragged on, life became less exciting. It seemed that people had battened down the hatches waiting for the spring, and I began to understand the term 'cabin fever'. So when Natasha and Meredith, my flatmates from Australia, arrived in London and suggested I join them on a driving tour around Britain, I jumped at the opportunity.

I wanted to ring Mum to let her know my plans. We hadn't spoken since before I went to Germany for Christmas and that phone call hadn't gone well. There was a weird formality about it and she didn't seem interested in my plans. She just re-iterated her words from before I left Sydney: that if I got stuck in Frankfurt she wouldn't send my Duchess dressing table. So now, when Dad answered the phone and told me Mum was out, I was relieved. I asked him to pass on the message that I'd call when I got back from my trip.

There is nothing like a month in a small car with two girlfriends to bash out a plan for your future. I was looking forward to having a captive audience to ponder my cross-cultural relationship. As it turned out, they both had their own cross-cultural relationships to ponder and I had to wait my turn.

As far as advice goes, I'm not sure how impartial we were, each enthusiastically supporting the other in her pursuit of love, perhaps to justify the pursuit of our own. We drove from morning till night each day, through England, Scotland and Wales, all the while discussing our respective lovers. Occasionally, we took time out from our navel-gazing to discuss world affairs and the likelihood of Armageddon. It was 1984 and the height of the Cold War. Tensions with the Eastern Bloc had reached new levels and newspapers were talking up the prospect that the final clash between good and evil was imminent. Berlin, still a divided city, seemed to feature as the trigger point.

So engrossed were we in our dual concerns of romance and the inevitable end of the world, we had to remind ourselves to observe our surroundings. Meredith read aloud from our guidebook and directed us to significant sights, but I was so pre-occupied that I absorbed only a vague sense of quaint English villages and woolly-tailed Welsh sheep and the expanse of the Scottish Highlands. However, importantly, we concluded that each of us had found fabulous men and that we should go for it.

On my return to London my flatmate Sinaed told me that Martin had rung from Germany three or four times that evening, so it was off to my grotty phone box on the corner, via the pub to get enough coins.

I dialled his number. The ringtone sounded muted and far away. He answered, announcing his surname in the German manner of telephone greetings. His mellow voice was somehow so grounding.

'Hi, it's me,' I said. 'I just got back. Sorry about the hour, but Sinead said it was important.'

'I have a proposition for you to think about, but I want you to say yes.'

'Okay. What is it?'

'I've been offered a job in West Berlin. I want to take it and I want you to come, too.'

'West Berlin! What about London? Can't they transfer you to London?'

'Not soon enough. This is a good job and West Berlin is a great city – historical, beautiful – you'd love it.'

I stopped myself from saying that Berlin would be the likely trigger point for Armageddon. There were other factors to be considered – the fact that I couldn't speak German, did not have a work visa, or a resident's visa for that matter, and had no way to earn money.

'Don't worry about the language. I'll teach you,' he said.

'We can make it work. Just say yes.'

That mellow voice again, so persuasive.

'Let me sleep on it.'

'I love you Mighty Big,' he said. I always felt as though my veins had been flushed with warm honey when he said that.

The next evening I met Natasha for dinner. As soon as we sat down I spilled the beans.

'West Berlin?' she said. 'Armageddon.'

'I know. And I don't speak German and I don't have enough money to last long without a job.'

'But you'll do it.'

I couldn't tell if it was a question or a statement, but in that moment, I knew that I'd go.

Far more worrying than the decision to move to the probable epicenter of the next world war was the thought of telling my parents – well, telling Mum. I knew this would send her into a spin – not the fact that we'd be living together, although she wouldn't be thrilled about that part either – but because it would confirm her worst fears that I'd never come home. Ever since the telegram episode before I left Australia, something had shifted. A block had developed that I found confusing, and any attempt I made to alleviate her concerns were dismissed.

My palms were sweating as I tried to manipulate the coins in my hand. I planned to call reverse charges, but the coins were a back-up. It was cold and my breath fogged up the phone booth. I dialled the number, my heart was thumping in my chest. Please don't let Dad answer the phone.

'Hello.'

'Oh. Hi, Dad.'

'Who's that?' Although I was his only daughter, Dad was never able to deduce that the female voice addressing him as 'Dad' was that daughter.

'It's me, Libby.'

'Libby! Where are you?'

'I'm still in London.'

'What time is it there?'

'About 10 o'clock. Could I please speak to Mum?'

'What's the weather like over there?'

'Still cold. Is Mum there?'

'Great to hear from you. Glad everything is going so well. I'll just get Mum.'

My heartbeat was pounding in my temples. It took an eternity for Mum to come on the line.

'Hello, Libby.'

'Hi, Mum. I have something to tell you. I'm moving to Berlin with Martin. He tried to get a transfer to London but it didn't work out, so we're both moving to Berlin.'

Silence.

'Mum?'

Silence.

My mind raced, canvassing all possibilities: she'd taken the news badly and would never speak to me again; she'd had a heart attack, died of shock right there at the other end of the phone line; or we had been cut off. The line was dead. But at what point in the conversation had that happened? How much had she heard?

I dialled again, my hands shaking so much I could barely manage it. I had no idea what mood to expect. The phone was ringing. I could hardly breathe.

'Hello.'

'Hi, Dad.'

'Who's that?'

'Dad, it's me again. Could I please speak to Mum?'

'Libby! What time is it there?' But the phone was taken out of his hand.

'Hi Libby. We were cut off. What were you saying?'

'That I'm moving to Berlin with Martin.'

'Moving to Berlin?'

'Yes. He's been offered a promotion and he's sick of Frankfurt. He says Berlin's a beautiful city.'

Silence.

'Mum?'

'Yes, I'm still here.'

'I'll be fine. And I'm definitely coming home. No doubt about it.'

'You might get stuck there.'

'I won't get stuck there.'

'When are you planning to move?'

'In a few weeks. I have to finish up this locum. Then I'll go.'

'But Mark's arriving in London in March. I told you that. He'll be so disappointed if he doesn't see you. I think he's having a bad time. He's said a few times how much he wants to see you.'

I suspected this was a ruse. She hadn't mentioned his plans before and there was no way of confirming them. He and his wife were travelling in the United States and then coming to Europe. In our last phone call he'd given no indication of his arrival dates or that he was having a bad time. It was now early February.

'When in March?'

'Probably early March. Maybe mid-March. I really think it's imperative that you wait for them.'

'I'll think about it. By the way, Martin says he'd love to see you again and to meet Dad.'

'I have to go. There's something boiling over on the stove.'

And that was it. I stood there in the phone box, now silent except for the pounding of my heart in my temples. I felt strange.

Elizabeth Lancaster

The wind had gone out of my sails and I was left wondering how long I'd have to wait for my brother to show up.

7. Café Kranzler

IT WAS STILL DARK when I left my London flat for the last time four weeks later to take the tube to Gatwick Airport. My brother had apparently stayed on in the United States and, apart from one letter from Mum with further references to my Duchess dressing table, there had been no acknowledgement of my plans. Once again, I went over in my head why moving to Berlin was a good idea. I hadn't seen Martin since Christmas and, in a moment of panic, thought I couldn't even remember what he looked like. That was ridiculous, of course. I opened my wallet and studied his photo. He looked back at me from his clear plastic compartment, steady as ever. Anyway, I could always come back to London. Maybe we could both move here at some point, if things worked out.

Martin was at Tegel Airport to meet me, full of enthusiasm for this magnificent city. As we left the airport in a taxi I peered through the windows, anxious to get a sense of my new surroundings. Martin's hype and my own pre-conceived ideas of glamour and cabaret did not fit with what I saw. Everything appeared to be enveloped in grey. Perhaps as we got closer to the city centre it would improve. We drove up the *Kurfürstendamm*.

'This is one of the most magnificent shopping avenues in Europe,' Martin announced, proudly.

I strained to see the beauty, but all I detected were drab, concrete box-like structures. Dead ahead of us was a sinister-looking scar of a building.

'What's that?' I asked.

'The *Gedächtnis Kirche*. It means Memory Church. It was almost destroyed at the end of the war, but it's been left as a reminder of what war brings.'

I shuddered. Everything I could see seemed to be a reminder of what war brings. Lego-style apartment blocks, hastily constructed to house a defeated people, filled the skyline. The once magnificent Ku'damm, as it's known, had perhaps thirty or forty of the original buildings along its entire length. The rest were more concrete boxes. Suddenly Martin asked the taxi driver to stop and we stepped out onto a busy intersection with all my bags.

'This is Café Kranzler,' he said, indicating a two-storey building with a festive red and white striped canopy which defied the bleak sky and freezing March morning.

'It is one of the most famous cafés in Europe.' He took my bags and we went inside. A waitress wearing a bitter expression showed us to a table upstairs.

Martin said something to her in German in his jaunty manner, which did not seem to impress her one bit, but he apparently didn't notice.

'Isn't it great?' he said to me once we were seated.

I knew I was tired, having had only a few hours' sleep the night before. Farewell drinks with work colleagues had been a late affair, followed by the excruciating four o'clock start to take the cheap flight to Berlin. I knew I should reserve my judgment.

The waitress was still standing there waiting for our order. Apart from the surly expression, there was something else unusual about her: her age, probably mid-fifties. She must be the owner, I thought. But when I looked around I noticed all the waitresses were the same – almost clones of each other – dyed blonde hair, severe expressions and in their fifties.

'*Bitte schön?*' she said impatiently, with her pad in hand.

Again her tone seemed lost on Martin. He responded cheerily and off she went. I assumed he had just ordered me a very strong coffee. She returned, however, carrying a tray with a bottle of champagne and two glasses. She set them down on the table, opened the bottle and poured. Martin put one in my hand, then leant forward and said earnestly, 'Are you awake?'

My eyes felt gritty from lack of sleep and my brain was foggy. The whole morning had had an other-worldly feel about it.

'I think so,' I said.

'Okay. Well … I just want you to know that wherever we go or whatever we do, I want you to be my wife.'

My mind lurched with an invisible double-take. How did we get to this? To something that sounded suspiciously like a marriage proposal.

'You don't have to say anything right away,' he said, perhaps in response to my stunned expression. 'I just wanted you to know.' Then he raised his glass and I raised mine, somewhat robotically.

What the hell was I doing here, drinking champagne in Café Kranzler on the *Kurfürstendamm* in West Berlin, fielding a marriage proposal?

After our confusing champagne interlude, Martin hailed another taxi. He explained that in West Berlin the pressure for accommodation was so acute that newcomers were often in a sort of holding pattern in temporary housing. As we approached the city's outskirts a massive grey structure came into view. My sense of foreboding grew as it became apparent that we'd reached our destination. Something reminiscent of a spaceship from *Star Wars* stood before us. Rigid grey tentacles fanned out in all directions from an ugly central body. A feeble attempt had been made to humanise it by painting the window frames bright yellow, a sad contrast to the endless cement.

Our tiny studio apartment was on the fourth floor. I looked out the window over miles of concrete. This was definitely not what I had expected.

'It's only until we find something more permanent,' said Martin.

The word 'permanent' rang in my ears. I thought of my flat in London, its proximity to Hyde Park and red double-decker buses and Harrods, or Sydney's blue skies and beaches. What was he thinking, tricking me into coming here with the lure of beauty and history? Did he think I might not notice that this was the ugliest place on the planet?

'I've booked you into a language school,' Martin said, cheerily. 'You'll go mad if you can't talk to anyone. You can start as soon as you like. Tomorrow, even. I'll help you learn in the evenings after work. The school is easy to get to with the *U-Bahn*.'

He unfurled a map onto the tiny laminex kitchen table. German maps are folded in a complex pattern of left over right, horizontal and vertical folds. Unless you are German it is impossible to ever get them back into their original configuration. He showed me where we were on the map (the north-west) and then pointed to the school's location (the south-east). Kreuzberg. He then produced the plan of the underground railway system – or *U-Bahn* – and highlighted where I should change trains. Then back to the original map to see how to get from the station to the school.

'German transport is very efficient,' he said. 'Not like in Downunder.'

I decided to start at the language school the next day. Martin would be at work, and I sure wasn't going to sit around here all day. So, armed with the origami map, I set off for Kreuzberg. I emerged from the *U-Bahn* to find a concrete jungle similar to the one I'd left thirty minutes earlier. I made my way to the Berliner Sprachen Institut, which was located on the first floor of a decrepit-looking building. It stood out from the rest in that it was a dull brown, rather than grey. A series of narrow corridors were choked by a bottleneck of students crowding around a coffee machine.

I was assigned to a beginner's class, where the lesson was already under way. I slipped in quietly and took a seat at the back. My teacher, tall and lean with thinning hair and a look of exasperation on his face, strode from one side of the classroom to the other, issuing incomprehensible instructions. He indicated where we were to look in the textbook, but it was of little help.

'*Ich springe,*' he said.

We sat there, impassively.

'*Ich springe,*' he repeated. This time accompanied by a little jump in the air. But we didn't make the connection.

'*Ich springe, ich springe, ich springe.*' Jump, jump, jump.

What the hell was he doing?

He walked over to the window and put one foot out, then leaned forward as if to leap to his death.

'*Ich springe aus dem Fenster!*'

Fenster. Now there was a word I recognised. Oh, I get it – he's going to jump out the window.

It was going to be a long, painful process to learn an entire language through a process of charades. Most days he didn't use actions to illustrate his point. He'd talk and look dejected at our lack of response. Most of the students were from various parts of Asia, so I couldn't even communicate with them in the break. So I'd just sit there for three hours a day and go home none the wiser. In the absence of anything else to do, I was very diligent with my homework and spent the remaining hours until Martin got home with a dictionary, learning vocabulary. I wrote out pages and pages of it and then tested myself.

When it came to constructing sentences, though, German was a mysterious language indeed. Word endings (and not just verbs) changed without apparent rhyme or reason. I'd ask Martin about it at night.

'Oh, don't worry about that. That's just an exception,' he'd say. I became increasingly suspicious as it happened in every sentence, but he was steadfast in his reassurance. 'German is full of exceptions.'

As Martin was also new to Berlin, our only social life was through his work functions – usually drinks on Friday evenings. Having been in Europe for over a year now, I was well used to being in situations where I did not speak the local language. But it was much more isolating to be without the language in a social situation. To be sitting with a group at something as ordinary as after-work drinks but unable to say even the simplest thing was somehow more disorientating than not understanding shopkeepers or even my German teacher.

To my ears, the German language sounded harsh. Occasionally, when someone spoke English to me, I found their directness disconcerting – like the time Martin and I invited one of his colleagues over for coffee.

'No, I do not think this would be possible,' she had said. 'I am too tired.'

No one I had ever met who spoke English would have offered such a weak excuse. Well, not really an excuse at all. Perhaps she just didn't like us. But the very next week, she invited us to her place for coffee. I began to question Australians' self-proclaimed reputation of being frank, open and direct. We didn't have a patch on the Germans.

My classes finished each day at lunchtime, so if I didn't feel like doing my homework, I had the afternoon to explore the city before Martin got home from work. There were museums and markets and a seventeenth century palace, which was open to the public. But the thing I found most fascinating of all was the Berlin Wall. I'd be on a bus, and at the most unexpected moments the Wall would burst into view as we rounded a corner. Given its significance, I had expected something of the magnitude of the Great Wall of China, but the Berlin Wall, celebrated in so many spy novels and movies, was surprisingly innocuous. If it were not for the graffiti sprayed on by West Berliners showing their contempt for the structure that artificially divided their city, I might have overlooked it altogether. Built of cement, it stood only about four metres high. It would have taken nothing to scale it and be off to freedom, but for the strategically placed guard towers on the Eastern side, permanently occupied by soldiers wielding machine guns, ready for the slightest sign of an escape.

Sometimes Martin and I went through to East Berlin, which was like stepping back in time forty years. The Wall from the Eastern side was pristine. The general population was not allowed within five hundred metres of it, so all the buildings within that no-go zone were now just empty shells with cracked windowpanes. In shopping squares, huge posters of Erich Hoenecker, East Germany's president, looked down Big Brother-style from billboards. People got about in their Trabants, tiny smoke-spewing cars that appeared not to have been updated since the war. After our day of sightseeing, I always wondered what the guards must have thought as they allowed us back through the checkpoint – that mysterious time machine that could return us to the modern era.

On long weekends everyone made for the *autobahns* to visit friends and family in other parts of West Germany, but the hours spent at the border while East German guards checked passports were excruciating. It seemed little more than an exercise in intimidation. How could so much animosity have grown up between people who were once unified? First they stared at the passport photo, then looked you in the eye, then back at the photo and again fixed your gaze. Back and forth it went between photo and face. If you dared glance away they barked orders to look at them. After finally establishing that you matched the photo in your passport they asked if you had any weapons or children on board. I was tempted to respond that the guns were in the boot and the twins were strapped under the car. Martin, usually so jovial, became nervous when I threatened to do this.

'These guys do not have a sense of humour. So unless you want to spend the night here being questioned, you won't say anything like that.'

Why would anyone choose to live here? I wondered.

My ambivalence about my new surroundings should have provided some comfort to my mother but I never got far enough in conversation to tell her about it. Her new, business-like approach prevented me from discussing anything more personal than my American Express bill, which was sent to her in Australia. I wondered why Mum and I were engaged in our own Cold War.

8. Phone Calls (ii)

AFTER A MONTH of painfully slow progress at language school, I was promoted to another class. My new teacher could not have been more different from the first. Compact, energetic, prematurely grey with a youthful face, he somehow broke through the barrier. As I was sitting in his classroom, it slowly dawned on me that I understood what he was saying. The words no longer ran together. It was as though a door to another world had been unlocked.

For a new player, one of the great advantages of German is the fact that there are virtually no exceptions (contrary to the great lie told by Martin) and that spelling and pronunciation are absolutely regular. Once you know the rules, you can read and pronounce just about any word put in front of you, whether you know it or not. This was my saving grace in my first job in Berlin as a *Tagesmutter* or day-nanny. Every day I had to collect six-year-old Jan from kindergarten, cook him *Bratwurst* for lunch and then keep him entertained until his mother arrived home from work at six o'clock. Fortunately, his favourite thing was to have me read his storybooks aloud. To begin with, I struggled to understand what I was reading, but Jan was unaware of my ignorance and I would piece it together from the pictures. And so gradually my vocabulary grew.

As my familiarity with the language increased, a curious thing happened: the harshness disappeared. It was replaced by a certain elegance that had not been apparent to my untrained ear. This was a strange transition, indeed. Surely the clash of harsh consonants, the guttural throat-clearing remained unchanged? Surely the *sound* was unchanged? Similarly, the unsettling directness that I had observed in conversation in English was not evident in German. Words were chosen for their precision and I delighted in discovering the subtleties and nuances of the language.

Now I couldn't get enough of it. I listened closely in order to emulate the cadence, the syntax and rhythms of the sentences. When I spoke, I worked hard to sound like a native speaker. If I heard another Australian speaking German, I'd cringe at the flatness of their accent, knowing that it probably reflected my own. When Martin got home in the evenings he'd often put his arms around me and say simply, '*Na, Du?*' I knew this was the familiar version of 'you' as opposed to the formal 'Sie', but now I also felt the intimacy of it.

On weekends Martin scoured the paper for accommodation. Eventually, he found an apartment in Charlottenburg, a short walk from the Ku'damm and *Schloss Charlottenburg*, the seventeenth century palace and jewel in West Berlin's crown. He applied for an interview, along with every other newcomer to Berlin, but luck was with us. The owners had spent a year in Queensland

and were enamoured with all things Australian, so we became the lucky winners of a spacious, furnished, fourth floor apartment *mit Balkon*. An apartment 'with balcony' is a prized possession in Berlin. The fact that it was so small you couldn't even put a chair on it didn't matter at all. We had our own bit of air space. The floor plan was a bit of a hotchpotch, oddly shaped nooks passing themselves off as bedrooms, but I had to admit, the wide open living area with high ceilings and parquetry flooring felt very grand.

Despite the tension between us, every now and then Mum would ring me. She only called when she knew Martin would be at work. Naturally, she never asked about him and I had learned not to raise him in the conversation. But one morning I decided to ring to tell her about the flat.

'The great thing is it's furnished and there's so much room.'

'Right. Well send me the address. By the way, we saw a dreadful truck accident on the news last night that happened somewhere in Germany.'

My stomach tightened. 'Don't worry, we don't have a car. Martin loves bike riding and Berlin's pretty flat.'

'Oh, I think there's something boiling over on the stove so I'd better go.'

'Mum, why is it something is *always* boiling over, when I ring you?'

'What? Look I have to go. I'll ring you later about your American Express bill.'

The American Express bill again. If I'd kept the conversation to that we could have spoken for fifteen minutes. I felt empty and flat after these calls.

I'm not sure how it happens, but in any large city foreigners manage to find each other. So in addition to my fellow students, Martin and I acquired various mixed nationality couples as friends. They formed the mainstay of our social life and we got together most weekends, or we might meet up with my teacher and other students in a pub in Kreuzberg and 'celebrate' until the small hours of the morning. Then we'd take a bus back to Charlottenburg, usually hopping off at an all-night *Imbiss* for a *Bratwurst* and hot chips. Thus far, we'd been a solitary act. Now, with a circle of friends, we had the opportunity to observe each other in a social context. Martin seemed to fit in effortlessly with whoever we met, his gentle manner quickly putting people at ease.

My early Café Kranzler shock notwithstanding, I came to appreciate the café culture of Germany, something that was still years away in Australia. Martin was a café afficionado and I loved watching him handle the abrasive Berlin career waitresses with his relentless cheerfulness. He'd place our order, then hold their gaze for just a moment longer than necessary and smile his warm, penetrating smile. Usually, they cracked and responded in kind. I wondered if it was a personal challenge he set himself to extract a smile from even the most serious type, but when I asked him, he had no idea what I meant. He hadn't even noticed their sour attitude. I was beginning to understand that we simply perceived the world differently.

Marzipan & Magnolias

In those early months, experiencing Berlin was like observing the transformation of a black and white film into colour, negative morphing into positive. As spring emerged, grey and khaki winter overcoats were replaced by bright spring fashions. The stark, giant plane trees that lined the Ku'damm now shimmered with new growth, softening the streetscape. Hints of Berlin's former glory began to reveal themselves.

I began to enjoy walking the length of the Ku'damm, with its wide footpaths and stylish shops. I'd study the facades and ornate finishes of surviving pre-war buildings, and try to imagine Berlin as it once was. On weekends, when we weren't engaging with café waitresses, we passed the time perusing English book stores or scouring the flea markets, or we might hop on the *U-Bahn* and head for Wannsee to hike around the lake and through the woods. Sometimes we'd take the bus to the Reichstag, which in the 1980s was unoccupied. The bus let us out on the edge of the vast lawn that led up to the building. Although it was not used during Hitler's reign of terror, having been destroyed by fires, it retained an eerie link to that period. Martin was always quiet on these excursions, and perhaps his confusion of emotions represented his generation: those who were born after the war, but felt the oppressive weight of its shadow nonetheless. Inside the Reichstag, right beside the Berlin Wall, was a small museum, which detailed the devastating chain of events that had resulted in this strange, compelling, divided city.

Every few months the engagement question popped up again, and each time I stalled. Everything was going so well, why complicate it with talk of marriage? There was, of course, the additional factor of where we would spend the rest of our lives, a detail that, thus far, we had only skirted around. It was just easier not to think about it, but the Immigration Department had other ideas. A crackdown on visa extensions meant that I had to leave. A letter arrived informing me of the bad news, and although I was not yet able to read German bureaucrat-ese, I recognised several words like jail and deportation. I rang Martin at work.

'Well there is a very easy solution,' he said.

'What?'

'Marry me.'

We had now been together in Berlin for nine months.

I knew I wouldn't leave without him, but I also knew I couldn't live there forever. I berated myself for getting into this situation. That night when Martin came home he announced that it was time.

'Time for what?' I said.

'To make a plan. If we get married and you want us to live in Australia, that's fine with me. It's a long way from Europe, but I don't suppose I'll find another koala like you around here.'

And that was it. Suddenly the decision was so simple, well not really a decision at all. We struck a deal with Immigration that they would extend my visa if we became formally engaged. My brother Mark and his wife Kim had at last appeared and were staying with us for a week. Martin's parents were also in Berlin for the weekend, so with representatives from both sides of the family, the timing to announce it officially was right.

Mark, with a glint in his eye, asked how we were going to break the good news to Mum. He was less sensitive to her disapproval and found his little sister's discomfort amusing. Discomfort was an understatement. The thought of a chilly response to our news both upset and infuriated me. Mark came up with the solution. Although we had never been a particularly traditional family, we could borrow from an old fashioned ritual: Martin would ring Dad to ask for my hand in marriage. As much as I bridled at the thought of having my hand asked for, and it seemed especially ludicrous since we'd been living together for the past nine months, I conceded that it was the best option.

We all huddled around the phone as Martin dialled their number in Sydney. I was so nervous. What if Mum answered? She'd be instantly suspicious if Martin asked to be put on to Dad. Ring ring, ring ring … They always took forever to pick up the phone. Finally a connection, the drama of the long distance pip, pip, pip before you could get started. I had my ear jammed beside Martin's on the receiver. Thankfully Dad answered.

'Hello.'

'Hello, Mr Lancaster, it's Martin here.'

'Who's that?' said Dad.

'Martin in Berlin.'

'Oh, Martin! How are you? Tell me, what time is it over there?'

'About eleven o'clock. Mr Lancaster, I want to ask you if I could have your daughter's hand in marriage. I love her very much.'

'What? Oh yes, yes. That's great news. When's the big day?'

At this point Mum took control of the receiver. But it was too late. The deal was done.

'Hello, Mrs Lancaster?' said Martin bravely. 'I love your

daughter very much. I promise to bring her back to Australia.'

'When?' said Mum. Her tone was brittle.

'As soon as possible.'

9. The Taste of Marzipan

AT CHRISTMAS WE BRAVED THE QUEUE at the East German border to visit Martin's parents on the island of Föhr in the North Sea, followed by a few days in his home town of Hamburg. Our hotel room overlooked the Alster, the magnificent lake, now frozen, which forms the centerpiece of Hamburg. Fresh snow covered the ground, and the sky was a brilliant blue.

There was something so intensely Christmassy about it all: a sea of scarves and beanies, festive markets, mugs of steaming *Gluhwein*, and hot candied almonds. As a child, it had never occurred to me that traditional Christmas carols did not, in any way, reflect my Australian experience. Singing about *dashing through the snow* in the searing heat, had not struck me as odd, but looking around me, it was as though I'd stepped into a children's picture book. I bought a pair of wooden angels to hang on a pot plant that doubled as a Christmas tree in our apartment.

One of my favourite festive treats was chocolate-coated marzipan, a specialty of Lübeck, near the Baltic Sea. I kept my stash in the hotel room and nibbled away at it between meals.

'You're going to turn into a piece of marzipan if you keep eating it at that rate,' Martin said when he spotted me unwrapping a piece shortly after breakfast. I popped it in my mouth anyway but it tasted strange and I spat it out. I tried another piece, but it had the same odd flavour and I spat it out too.

'This tastes really weird,' I said. 'Try a piece.'

He tasted a corner of the piece I handed him.

'It seems alright to me,' he said.

I took it back and put it in my mouth.

'Yuk!' I spat it out. 'It tastes sort of *dead*!'

Martin looked puzzled. I took a bite from an apple, but it had the same bizarre, dead flavour. I brushed my teeth, but even the toothpaste was awful.

'This is so strange,' I said. 'I just won't eat anything for a while.'

'I warned you about eating so much marzipan.'

Later we met up with old friends of Martin's at a café. I was wary about trying the cake after the morning's events. Placing a small piece on my tongue, I knew immediately the problem was still there. I tried to swallow it quickly, but that too was now difficult. It required all my concentration to force the muscles in the back of my throat to work together. They simply would not coordinate. As the weakness in my throat progressed so did my level of panic. My mind raced, canvassing possible causes. From my hospital experience, I began to suspect it was a neurological problem. I just wanted to get out of there but there was no way to signal this to Martin who was already ordering another round of coffee for everyone. So I sat patiently, not eating or drinking or speaking.

'You were quiet,' said Martin when we finally left. 'What's wrong?'

I described my symptoms but I could tell he didn't understand the seriousness. I dreaded the drive back through East Germany and the inevitable tussle with the border guards to reach West Berlin. My imagination did its worst, presenting me with every dreadful scenario during the two-hour car trip. On our return we called a friend who was studying medicine. He sounded concerned and advised us to go straight to the hospital.

I was seen by the neurology registrar, who was intrigued by my case. After much discussion and examination, he assessed my ability to taste by dipping a cotton bud into various substances and placing it on my tongue. I'd seen patients undergo this test during ward rounds, as a demonstration for medical students. It revealed that I had no sense of taste on the right side at all, and my ability to swallow on that side was completely absent. The doctor was curious.

'I have never seen this before,' he said. 'It is a paralysis of the ninth cranial nerve. One does not usually see this nerve paralysed in isolation. Perhaps it is due to a virus.'

He asked me to return the next morning to appear before a panel of neurologists. This tested my German to the limit as I answered questions fired in rapid succession. They took turns looking in my mouth and pressing the back of my throat with a long cotton tip to confirm that I really had no gag reflex. The professors conferred in low tones and then delivered their verdict: that my symptoms were most probably the result of a virus on the nerve, and should resolve. There was the outside possibility of a more serious cause, like multiple sclerosis.

This news arrived like a ton of bricks in my stomach. Images of Venus, my first patient from St Vincent's, and her squeaky wheelchair, suddenly loomed large before my eyes. I willed myself to block her out.

'What if the doctors are wrong?' I said to Martin when we left the consulting room. 'What if it's not a virus?'

'Don't worry. A whole room full of brain doctors couldn't be wrong. But maybe you should stay away from marzipan for a while.' He put his arm around me and we walked out into the bracing Berlin morning.

The thought of eating now filled me with dread. The loss of taste was creepy and swallowing was hard work. Mealtimes served as an unwelcome reminder of my symptoms, reigniting my fear that this was more than a virus on the nerve, but Martin encouraged me to try to eat normally. The muscles on the left side of my throat were still working so if the mouthfuls were small and I kept the food on that side of my mouth I could manage. After several weeks I began to detect an improvement – a hint of flavour, some power in the back of my throat. I was reviewed frequently by the neurology registrar during that month and gradually things returned to normal, just as he'd predicted. Martin and I were now planning our move to Australia and I convinced myself that all I needed was a good dose of sunshine.

10. The Dress Looks Lovely

IT WAS MY TWENTY-FIFTH BIRTHDAY and a perfect summer's morning when I arrived back in Sydney. Even through aircraft fumes, I detected the familiar coastal scent – a heady mix of sea salt, heat and humidity.

The practical logistics of moving countries for the two of us hadn't been as complex as I'd expected. My possessions could be squashed into a backpack and one additional suitcase. Martin only wanted to bring his books, golf trophies, and, of all things, some champagne glasses ('think of all the celebrating we could do Downunder'). We packed everything into cardboard boxes one weekend and taped them closed. While Martin was at work, a friend collected me in his VW Beetle. Like clowns in a Mini Minor we jammed ourselves and the boxes into the car and headed for the post office. So with a few stickers warning 'fragile' and some postage stamps, Martin's life was packed up and shipped to Australia. I flew ahead of him to organise accommodation and a car, and to resume my old job back at St Vincent's Hospital.

I rang Mum to let her know I was coming home but said she didn't need to worry about coming to the airport.

'Oh, I couldn't,' she said. 'I'd be at work.'

The now familiar knot in my stomach tightened. I wondered how our relationship had become so strained.

Instead, Natasha met me at the airport and we headed straight to our old flat. She had picked up a birthday cake for me and now busied herself with the kettle and coffee mugs. It felt strange. On the one hand so familiar: the brown flecked carpet (even in the kitchen), the tiny pre-war water heater above the sink. On the other hand, it felt as though I was viewing everything through the wrong end of a telescope – real but not real.

Natasha handed me a coffee and slice of carrot cake.

'So, happy birthday,' she said, raising her coffee mug by way of a toast. 'And to think you're engaged. *Engaged*! Did you know your Mum put a notice in the paper about it?'

'No, she didn't tell me,' I said. 'She doesn't make reference to it – it's as if I've been living over there by myself.'

'She'll come around. She rang me three times to check I'd be at the airport on time.'

We sat there in our old kitchen for several hours drinking one cup of coffee after another until it was time for me to go home. I felt almost sick with nerves.

Natasha dropped me off and I made my way to the front door ready to face Mum on my own. She must have been watching out for me because she was already at the door. We sort of looked at each other. Then she gave me a peck on the cheek, as if I'd only been gone for a week.

'How was the flight?'

'Fine. How are you and Dad?'

'Fine. Would you like to have a shower?'

She looked different. Older, as though more than two years had passed. And her expression was distant or anxious. I couldn't tell which.

'The boys are all coming over for dinner tonight, if you're not too tired.'

'No, that's great.'

I dumped my bags in my old room and had a shower. Dad arrived home shortly afterwards and was, as usual, oblivious to any subtle undercurrents in the house.

'Libby! How was the flight? Probably a 747. And Martin, when's he arriving?'

'About six weeks.'

'I'll make some tea,' said Mum and retreated to the kitchen.

I rarely mentioned Martin in conversation with Mum because my efforts were met with a response equivalent to rice boiling over on the stove. She was, however, strangely determined to put on a fabulous wedding. And I was strangely reluctant to be involved in her preparations.

'What about getting married at the church up here on the corner? It's lovely and convenient for everybody.'

'I don't know that we want to get married in a church. We're not religious.'

'Don't be silly – you don't need to be religious. It's what people *do*. So much nicer than one of those awful celebrants. Why don't I make a tentative booking for the second Saturday in May?'

'We won't be getting married in May. Martin is only arriving in April.'

'But...'

'There's no way we're getting married in May.'

'Okay. I'll book the church for the second Saturday in September.'

Mum was right. We had to get onto it. Martin was entering the country on an 'engagement' visa which meant we had to be married within six months of his arrival. I wasn't sure whether I was arcing up against Mum or the Immigration Department. My preference would have been to spend time with Martin in Sydney, establish a life for ourselves and move at out own pace.

I thought about the last wedding we'd been to in Berlin only a month earlier. The couple got married in a registry office and then we'd somehow ended up having snow fights at the Berlin Wall as East German guards observed us from their tower. After that we'd returned to their apartment and celebrated with *Gluhwein*. There'd been no fuss, no finery. No one over the age of thirty had attended. In fact, now that I thought about it, I had never met any of our German friends' parents. I don't think they had parents. It was a whole city of under-thirties. Maybe I was more bohemian at heart than I'd ever realised.

My first task was to find a place for us to live, so while still in the grip of jetlag I approached real estate agents in the Neutral Bay area near my old flat. At that time Sydney had nothing like the housing shortage we'd experienced in Berlin, so within a few hours I had secured a two-bedroom apartment within walking distance from the ferry. I could move in right away.

Work was my refuge. I returned to Ward 17, where my colleagues seemed satisfied with vague responses about wedding plans. Travelling to and from work was a daily pleasure. Leaving my flat in the mornings and walking down to the ferry wharf – salty air clinging to my bare legs – was still a huge novelty after a long Berlin winter. There was something soothing about the air and the chug-a-lugging of the ferry.

The neurology ward was much the same as when I'd left. Although after my recent experience on the wrong side of a neurological encounter, I decided to switch to orthopaedics or outpatients – any other specialty – at the first opportunity.

I missed Martin. Six weeks was a long time to be separated but we wrote many letters. His were immediately recognisable with his large uppercase handwriting on the envelope. They were short but consistent in their message: his confidence in our decision and our future was rock-solid. This steadied me. And twice a week we spoke on the phone.

'I miss you. I just can't wait to leave here now and get to Downunder.'

'I miss you too. I really wish you were here. Mum's in full wedding mode. She thinks we should get married in a church near their house.'

'Sounds good. Is it nice?'

'I don't know. It's sandstone with a slate roof. It's quaint from the outside.'

'Perfect.'

'Do you really want to get married in a church?'

'Why not? It fits the occasion, don't you think?'

'I was thinking about Volker and Maria's wedding at the Berlin Wall. It was no fuss. I liked that.'

'That's Berlin, but I want to do this properly. It's important.'

With lobbying from Mum and Martin the church wedding became inevitable. With that box ticked, Mum moved on to the next item on the list, and then the next. There were guest lists to be drawn up, invitations to be printed, fabric to be chosen, a photographer to be booked and, of course, the house to be prepared for a wedding. Mum was energy itself, darting here and there to compare prices or interview some prospective service provider.

'When Martin gets here, perhaps you two could paint the inside of the garage – that's where the dance floor will be. I've ordered the marquee for the driveway. It seats ninety. That should be fine, unless many of Martin's relatives decide to come.'

Eventually, Martin arrived in Australia, and with his usual glass-half-full world-view he was thrilled with Mum's wedding arrangements, barely noticing that she barely noticed him. Her questions were confined to practical issues, like, 'We're organising the catering for the wedding. Do your parents eat seafood?' But he was unfazed.

'She has to look after her only daughter's interests,' he said to me later. 'I'd do the same thing.'

There was almost a last minute hitch in the arrangements when the Church ministers' rosters were unexpectedly altered and our wedding service was allocated to the more senior of the two. He was reluctant to join us in holy matrimony when he learned i) we were already living together (in the biblical sense), and ii) we were not 'of the parish' or ever likely to be. Mum was outraged by his hypocrisy.

'He calls himself a Christian,' she thundered, furious that he would even consider refusing us.

I pointed out that technically we were the hypocrites, not him. However, in a moment of generosity, he agreed to overlook this breach in the rules (which for some reason had not disturbed his colleague) when he learned the invitations had been sent. The crisis was averted.

And so we moved inexorably towards the Big Day.

Meredith, who had become something of a wizard seamstress, offered to make my dress. Despite my foot-dragging approach to most aspects of this wedding, the dress managed to rope me in. It was ankle-length ivory pink Thai silk with rows of fine pintucks down the front to the waist and millions of tiny buttons down the back.

A few nights before the wedding, I called in to my parents to finalise the guest seating arrangements with Mum. As we argued the toss over who should sit beside Great Aunt Florrie, Mum casually mentioned that if there were ever any problems with Martin I could always come back home.

'Why would there be any problems?' I asked.

'Well, Marion Johnson's niece married a German and he used to bash her.'

'Mum!'

'I'm just saying, if he ever lays a finger on you, just walk out the door. Don't take it.'

'Martin isn't like that. Surely you can see that.'

'You can't always tell. Old Chester used to say – and he fought in the War – that you just couldn't tell with them. Although, he actually thought we should have been fighting the French – very arrogant, the French.'

'Right. Well, I think I'll go now. I still have a lot to do.'

She walked me to the door.

'Anyway, the dress looks lovely on you.'

No one on the day would have guessed at my resistance to all the formality. In addition to my stunning dress, I had not one but a trio of bridesmaids to match Martin's groomsmen. (He couldn't pick between the three close friends he had in Australia.) However, I put my foot down at hiring fancy cars to transport us the short distance between my parents' house and the church. Instead, we walked. Traffic passing our little party honked their horns and complete strangers hooted out of car windows.

The church with its vaulted ceilings and sandstone walls gave the sense of occasion Mum and Martin were after. As I entered with Dad, I saw Martin waiting at the other end. He looked so proud and chuffed, and I felt the smile on my face broaden. Even the dour minister seemed to have cheered up for the event.

Vows were exchanged, hymns were sung and marriage certificates signed in a euphoric blur. We sailed back up the aisle to Mendelssohn's 'Wedding March' playing at full throttle.

'You did it,' whispered Martin as we stood at the top of the church steps, confetti landing all around us (in contravention of Church Rules).

'*We* did it,' I said, leaning into him as he put his arm around me. It all felt perfect. Martin, Mum, the Immigration Department had been right all along.

On the return walk to my parents' house, our wedding party was joined by ninety guests. Once again cars beeped and honked as they passed.

Martin's father, Erich, gave a speech in English, which he had obviously spent much time perfecting as he over-enunciated every syllable with alarming contortions of his mouth. Helga, Martin's mother, then stood up and, speaking no English, rattled off a short, impromptu speech in German. She then raised her glass and threw back her champagne. She was standing only a metre from my father and facing in his direction. Dad feared that she intended to throw the glass, as they do in European movies after skolling a shot, and dived for cover. However, there was no such show of passion, and Helga sat down quietly, while my father tried to think of a plausible explanation for his defensive action.

The dancing began and Erich graciously asked Mum to dance. There was an initial power struggle about who was leading but after a few turns they seemed to find a rhythm. I knew the night had exceeded Mum's wildest expectations when she tipped the disc jockey five dollars. She sat down beside me and, leaning in, put her arm around me.

'It's good to have you back,' she said.

11. The Magnificent

A YEAR TO THE DAY after Martin's arrival in Australia we moved into our very own little semi-detached house in Sydney's inner-city. We had bought it at auction six weeks earlier, and during that time I often walked there after work, just to admire it from the outside. It was owned by an elderly woman named Edith Match who lived there with her companion, Joan. After the auction Edith congratulated us on 'winning'. For some reason she'd taken a shine to Martin, although they had never met before.

'I said to Joan, "I hope that young man and his wife win the house." And you did, God bless you. I said, "Joan, they'll be able to do the place up a bit." She doesn't want to move, but what can you do?'

Joan was standing about a metre behind Edith and shuffled from side to side.

'Don't worry,' I said. 'We'll look after it very well.'

'Of course you will. I told Joan that.'

The day before settlement, I was once again marvelling at our future home from the footpath opposite, when Edith spotted me. She called out for me to come inside. There were boxes everywhere and a sad mood hung in the air. Edith ushered me past the boxes, along the hall and into the kitchen, while Joan remained a shadowy figure, gliding between the bedrooms.

'We've collected so many things, Joan and I, over the years – too much to take with us. Would you and your lovely husband have any use for this cabinet, dear? It has excellent storage space. Joan wants to take it with us, but she's unrealistic about how much room we'll have in the new place.'

We knew from the estate agent that they were moving into a retirement village, but Edith never mentioned the term. I looked at the 1940s-ish crockery cabinet nestled into an alcove in the kitchen, with little doors at the top containing bubble glass and wobbly brass handles.

'We'd love the cabinet,' I said. 'Just leave anything you don't have room for.'

The next day we took possession of our first house. It was a miniature Federation, so it had the trademark hallway with luxuriously high ceilings, elaborate cornicing and ceiling roses. An arch in the hall and a fireplace in the living room added a stately air to my doll's house. However, moving through to the kitchen, things changed from stately home to country cottage. There was no running water or sink in the kitchen, which consisted of a Kelvinator fridge, left by Edith, and an ancient oven and stove, set side by side at a height appropriate for fairytale characters. Running water was only available from the laundry, which contained huge cement tubs. But these small inconveniences bothered me not at all. The pièce de résistance was the pocket handkerchief square of buffalo grass out the back – our very own patch of Australia.

Edith had, indeed, left the cabinet in its little alcove. I wrestled the door open to look inside. It was empty apart from a very old, pale blue cardboard box, fastened with string. There is something romantic about boxes tied with string, in the same way that Central Station or the airport departure gate is romantic. I removed the string with great anticipation to discover an odd collection of bits and pieces: a set of tarnished silver salad servers with cut glass handles, a butter knife with a broken mother-of-pearl handle (all the pieces still there, as if awaiting repair) and a set of sugar tongs. I tried to imagine Edith and Joan sitting together in their quaint kitchen, using the silver sugar tongs; I wondered whether Edith had been cross when Joan broke the mother-of-pearl knife. Perhaps she'd dropped it on the cement laundry floor, then carefully gathered up the scattered pieces, thinking she'd get it fixed. I do that – I keep bits of things for years, telling myself that I'll get them fixed, secretly knowing that I'll never get around to it. I closed the box and returned it to the cabinet.

I contemplated the different stages of our lives – Edith and Joan would probably always think of this as their house. Despite Edith's brave face, she could be forgiven for resenting the interlopers who could hardly wait to pull down her carefully chosen light fittings from the 1960s, rip up layers of cracked lino and threadbare carpets, and organise plumbing to the kitchen at the earliest opportunity. Soon, apart from Edith's cabinet (and blue box), there would be little evidence that this had been their home for the best part of fifty years.

I kept walking from one end of our little house to the other. I was certain that I would never need more than this for as long as I lived.

Within months of moving in, bohemian Berlin seemed like a distant memory as we began work on the house. Weekends were spent sanding, spak-filling, painting, arguing over colours and then repainting. Mid-way through the re-building, when the bathroom was gone and the back wall of the house was just a tarpaulin, I discovered I was pregnant. We no longer had access to a proper toilet and when morning sickness threatened, the thought of using the porta-loo was hideous enough to allow me to suppress it. Then bad weather began in earnest. Horizontal sheets of rain drove into the kitchen until the floor was several inches under water. Edith's cabinet took the brunt of it. Once the water and mud had receded, we inspected the damage. It was swollen and stinking. I prised open one of the doors to find the shelves had collapsed.

'Can you guide me while I drag this out to the footpath?' asked Martin. 'Someone would probably be glad to take it away.'

We lugged it out, carelessly bumping the legs as we manoeuvred it down the front steps to the footpath. I felt guilty as we dumped it there, but I knew neither of us had the time or inclination required to repair it. I removed the blue cardboard box, miraculously dry, and took it back inside with me.

After months of building work, including connecting running water to the kitchen, our house was ready. The final challenge was to shoe-horn my Duchess dressing table into our bedroom. Mum thought we didn't have enough room but if placed at an angle in the corner, I thought it looked most impressive.

Within weeks our first child was born, a son, Max. Like all new parents we honestly believed that our baby was the most beautiful ever born. I was surprised at how easily I took to motherhood; it helped that Max was one of those babies that fed easily and slept a lot. Martin loved becoming a dad, and behaved as if he were the first man ever to have achieved such a feat. He planned a new outing each weekend: the park, the zoo, the promenade at the beach, Martin pushing the stroller all the way.

Mum was also thrilled at the arrival of her first grandchild and saw him as often as possible. One day when she and Dad were visiting she glanced at the space that had once been occupied by Edith's cabinet.

'I think our piano would fit in that spot,' she said.

'Really?' I said.

'Yes. It's important for Max to grow up with one in the house. John, could you get the tape measure out of the car?'

My parents never travelled anywhere without a tape measure. Who knew when you might need to measure up for a new door or shelving or a piano?

It turned out to be an exact fit and Mum organised for it to be delivered. It was an upright with elaborate brass candlesticks and the word *Ronisch* inlaid in gold lettering above the music stand. I was chuffed with my acquisition. As a child I'd always wished I had learned the piano instead of the violin. Who unpacks their violin just to play a quick tune when they're in the mood? Instead of practising pieces for the school orchestra, I'd sit at the piano, and laboriously make my way through sheet music of popular songs, teaching myself as much as I could.

There was a narrow strip of grass between the house and the front fence. Not enough space to do anything with, so Mum suggested a feature tree.

'What about a magnolia?' she said. 'They are magnificent trees and very hardy. A soulangiana would work well in that spot.'

'Wouldn't a magnolia be too big?'

'No. It would be magnificent.'

We went to nurseries together in the winter so we could see them in bloom. Colours and sizes varied enormously, and we weighed the pros and cons of each, but in the end it was decided that the medium-sized soulangiana with its traditional pink flowers was probably the best. When we brought it home Martin was prevailed upon to dig a hole and, like planting a flagpole in the soil of a newly discovered country, we officially laid claim to our land.

In order to appreciate the full effect of our new acquisition, the three of us walked out onto the footpath and looked back toward the house. In the process of planting, the petals had fallen off and all that remained was a bare trunk about one-and-a-half metres high with a few stick branches.

'It really will be magnificent,' said Mum.

Martin and I began to refer to it as the Magnificent.

'Did you see the Magnificent is getting leaves?' Martin said one day. Or, 'Have you watered the Magnificent recently?'

Marzipan & Magnolias

Mum also gave me several roses to plant out the back – thornless and safe for children, but as hardy and forgiving as the magnolia out the front. Although I'd grown up in a true gardener's garden, before now I'd never thought about how I'd want my own garden to look. I'd never even realised it was important to me. Mum had a vast array of unusual specimens from all over the country, and now cultivated cuttings for me.

I began to pop into nurseries with Max. It helped if there was a pond with goldfish and lilies to amuse him, leaving me free to ponder my purchases. Almost everything I bought was inappropriate for the spot for which it had been selected, requiring either more sun, more shade, more water or better soil. Anything that did survive had to be resilient enough to withstand eager little fingers, wanting to pick the 'pretty flowers', roots and all.

Before we bought the house Martin had declared his lack of interest – even aversion – to gardening. That hadn't worried me unduly at the time, and in any case, I was sure that eventually I'd be able to turn him around. For now, though, he was remaining true to his word. So between his avoidance behaviour and Max's inadvertent destruction, establishing a garden proved to be a constant source of frustration to me.

Within a few years, though, the Magnificent out the front was compensating for my lack of progress, punching above its weight and giving every illusion of an established garden beyond.

When Max was two, our daughter Amy was born, over whom we were equally besotted. Having grown up in a household of boys, I was overjoyed about having a girl, secretly thrilled at the prospect of pretty dresses and hair ribbons. Max did not share our enthusiasm for the new addition to the family and made his displeasure plain as only a toddler can. There was no six-week honeymoon period, promised by the parenting magazines. From the beginning, Max seemed to understand that his life would never be quite the same again.

Amy's arrival coincided with Martin's job becoming more demanding, with longer hours, and over the next twelve months life became increasingly hectic. Our tiny semi, which had been perfect for the two of us, was bursting at the seams with four. It was so small that if Martin took his shoes off in the living room it was too crowded, and Max badgered me from the moment he woke up each morning to take him to the park to chase birds. If I used delaying tactics, he chased Amy instead. Around and around my legs they went as I'd try to pick up toys that booby-trapped doorways, threatening to trip me at every turn. I was working part-time at both St Vincent's and Sydney Hospital and Martin was now travelling to the United States frequently for work. I found it difficult being on my own so often with such young children and Max missed him terribly. As much as we loved our little house, I thought if there was a garden for the kids, life would be easier.

Almost by accident, when I was visiting my parents in Sydney's north, I came across a dilapidated 1920s weatherboard cottage with a rambling garden and lots of trees. It was a 'renovator's delight' and further from the city than we'd ever intended to live, but I absolutely fell in love with it. I begged Martin to come and see it. When he arrived, it was clear from his expression before he even got out of the car that he thought I had lost my mind.

'Please tell me you're not serious,' he said.

But he was unprepared for my almost evangelical commitment to the idea. I man-handled him out of the car and walked him around the property, giving a running commentary on all the wonderful things we could do with it. In the space of a few hours, I had reshaped our next five-year plan. Martin's arguments about being so far from the city, his anxiety about the size of the lawn he'd have to mow and the decrepit state of the house cut no ice with me. I sermonised on the benefits for the children of fresh air and space to run around, and made baseless promises that I would mow the lawn myself. Fortunately there was one selling point for him: it had a lock-up garage with a remote control. It must have been the first remote control ever produced, but the idea of gliding into his own car space at night instead of driving around for twenty minutes to find a spot appealed to him enormously. The deal was done and with barely a backward glance we left our doll's house semi behind and headed north.

Our new home was an adventure playground for the children. The central rooms of the house all opened onto a wraparound verandah, enclosed on two sides. Max and Amy quickly discovered you could run circuits of the house, disappearing through one door and miraculously reappearing through another, like the chase scenes in Tom and Jerry cartoons. The garden was a wild affair with nooks and crannies providing unlimited hiding places. Amy was now old enough to be useful to Max as a character or prop in his make-believe games. I enrolled Max in a local pre-school and

Amy in a playgroup. Although the house was in urgent need of work, the sheer space around us felt luxurious.

Mum was delighted to have us close by and called in most days – usually fleeting visits as she'd rush through my new house with quick instructions on this or that. She had an opinion on everything from the children's dentist to our curtain fabric. She offered to collect Max from pre-school when I was at work and was our chief babysitter on weekends. The granny in the track pants and K-mart sneakers, Martin called her. He never got used to the fact that you didn't sit down and chat with Mum. She was either up a ladder painting, or elbow-deep in potting mix.

'Libby,' she'd say, waving fistfuls of fabric swatches, 'there's a plaid on sale at Discount Fabrics that would be perfect for your sofa.'

'I was considering a yellow and white stripe I saw the other day. It looked so fresh.'

'No, that won't work with kids. You need an all-over pattern that won't show the dirt.'

If she observed me fumbling with the pinch pleats as I tried to make curtains, she'd step in to correct my mistakes.

'Oh, it's dreadful to have such a hopeless daughter,' she'd say light-heartedly, as she positioned herself at my sewing table, from where she could view my garden. 'Those roses need to be fertilised. I'll send your father over later to do it. I'll get him to prune them properly, too. You have to cut on an angle just above the leaf joint, you know.'

Our new property had previously been a market garden and

still had many rows of thorny rose bushes. They all had to be pulled out and new garden beds dug. Mum involved herself in the project with great enthusiasm, drawing on advice from her many contacts in the gardening world and passing it on to me. Often we went to nurseries together. It was uncanny how our taste in plants overlapped. We could both love or hate any given plant with unnatural passion. Sometimes we might wander through a nursery separately, then meet at the cash register with an identical selection of plants in our trolleys.

'It's genetic,' Mum would say. 'Aunt Alice would have chosen the same things.'

I became passionate about gardening. Looking out over my unruly property, I began to see what hadn't been apparent before. There was an intrinsic structure to it just waiting to be realised. In my mind's eye, there were now pebble pathways winding through a shady glen, stone steps cut into a grassy embankment and a grove of snow pears in the sunshine. I found myself sketching plans for the garden. Needless to say, Martin was not quite as excited about my ideas, as he knew I'd be trying to recruit him as my labourer on weekends. It was our one source of friction. Mum, however, could not have been happier with my new-found interest.

So when we learned three years later that Martin was to be transferred to the United States, I knew there'd be trouble.

12. The Piano

IT WAS NEW YEAR'S EVE 1994 when the news of Martin's transfer came through. We were sitting with friends on our verandah having a drink when head office in Germany rang announcing his almost immediate move to New York. Well, *our* move to New York.

When the possibility had first been raised some months earlier, I agreed with such haste I'd shocked myself. But it had always been a long shot, requiring the successful purchase of another company in Manhattan. In recent times the deal appeared to have fallen through, so this phone call was completely unexpected.

The evening then took on a momentum of its own. Champagne was poured, toasts were proposed, impromptu speeches were made about how we'd be missed. I put on a Sinatra CD and *New York, New York* echoed across the neighbourhood. We danced and sang until we were hoarse. When everyone finally left, Martin and I flopped onto the outdoor chairs. It was a warm, cloudless night and cicadas trilled away with unbridled enthusiasm, as if trumpeting the news of our imminent departure.

My sense of adventure didn't last long, though, when I

remembered Mum. I'd mentioned the possibility to her, but had played it down because it had seemed so unlikely. Now, the thought of facing her made me feel weak. No doubt, I'd be put in the freezer again.

Martin went to bed but I knew that I wouldn't be able to sleep so I collected glasses and empty bottles, back and forth, loading and unloading trays. The rhythm of the work blanked my mind. Just before I went to bed, I sat down at the piano and tried to pick out Sinatra's song on the yellowed keys, wishing for the five thousandth time in my life that I'd learnt to play properly. I managed the first few phrases and kept playing them over and over.

In the morning I drove to my parent's house. As I turned into their driveway my mouth was dry. I could see Mum from the car, perched up on a ladder, painting the architraves. She was wearing a spattered tracksuit, a walking record of all the colours she'd ever painted walls or woodwork throughout my life. Her glasses and grey hair were sprinkled with paint. Seeing me she'd climbed off the ladder. She could tell something was up.

'Mum, that transfer to New York has come through. It's pretty sudden – we have to be there in a few weeks.' My words shot out like bullets. She looked straight at me. Her unmade-up face was tight-lipped and severe.

'For how long?'

'Four years.' The sound echoed off the walls. 'I know it will be hard for you and Dad, and us too – but it's a big opportunity for Martin.'

'Yes. Well, this was bound to happen one day.' She studied her hands, trying to rub the paint flecks away.

'Mum, I can come home straight away if you need me – if anyone got sick …'

'Why would I tell you if we got sick? What would be the point?'

A breeze scattered the newspapers that had been spread to protect the verandah floxor. She bent to rearrange them and then climbed back up the ladder and continued painting.

New York, Martin had always said, would be his ultimate challenge. I had thought it would be mine too, but now my confidence was faltering.

Mum continued to come over once or twice a day but her demeanour was grim. She wouldn't stay, but she couldn't stay away.

'I'm taking these curtains home to finish. Your chair makes my back ache.' Then she'd disappear, leaving me to wonder how we'd ever get past this.

Then there was the piano. I was completely blindsided when Mum marched through my front door one day carrying armloads of curtains, and said, 'Don't bother sending that old piano back to our place. Your father and I will have moved into something smaller by the time you get back from America and we won't have room for it.'

'We'll take it with us,' I said.

'No, pianos don't travel well. It would be ruined. Just get rid of it.' She thrust a newspaper advertisement into my hand: *$250 for pianos sight unseen.* I just looked at her, dumbfounded. Her mouth was drawn into a thin line and in that moment I knew I didn't have the reserves to fight her.

I called the number in the ad. When the man arrived he couldn't believe his luck. 'Take it away, boys,' he said as he shoved the crisp bills into my hand. As I watched the Ronisch carted away I felt sick. I took the money over to Mum's to get rid of it as quickly as possible. She was in the kitchen trimming thorns off freshly cut roses. Her fingers displayed the usual array of scratches and Band-Aids. I held out the money to her but she didn't look up.

'What do I want with $250?' she said flatly. 'It was your piano, it's your money.'

My piano! I wanted to shout and scream that it was her piano that she had just sold. If it were my piano, I would not have sold it. I would never have sold my piano. I felt like such a fool, but it was all too late.

'Are you going to treat me like this for four years?' I asked.

'Yes, probably. It might be the only satisfaction I get.'

Her eyes met mine momentarily.

For a moment I thought I saw a ghost of a smile. I thought that the impasse was broken. But just as suddenly the veil closed over again. The money had formed a tight ball in my hand. I dropped it on the kitchen table and walked out.

I found Dad sitting on their front verandah, sanding back a coffee table Mum wanted restored. Sweat dripped off his forehead.

'She takes no prisoners, does she?' I said.

He looked up briefly. 'No, she doesn't.'

The day of departure was approaching. I was terrified to leave with so much tension between us.

'The first six months will be the hardest,' I said when I dropped in with the kids one afternoon.

'Oh, yes. After six months it could just as easily go on forever.'

'Look, Mum, I don't think it's a good idea for you and Dad to come to the airport.'

'Well, we are coming. How do you think we'll fill in the day wondering if you've left yet?'

So there we were in the smoke-filled bar at Sydney Airport staring at our coffee. Even Martin struggled to fill the silences. We kept asking unnecessary questions – did they have change for the car park, petrol to get home. No one mentioned tomorrow.

The strain in my voice went unnoticed by the children. They were just thrilled to be at an airport. Dad took them over to the huge windows where they could watch planes taxiing in to line up with the giant caterpillar-like walkway that we would soon be entering. Dad loved airports too, and could happily lose himself in the fantasy of fighter pilots and war heroes, for a while oblivious to the reason we were all there.

Mum sat stiffly in The Outfit she always wore for important occasions: a blue, pleated skirt, plaid cardigan and crisp, white blouse. She always looked like someone else's mother when she wore The Outfit, not the No Frills granny in track pants and sneakers.

I felt sick as I watched the second hand of a giant wall clock sweep inexorably forward. I wished that time would stop dead, while desperately willing this moment to be behind us. At last it was time.

'Come and say goodbye, kids,' I called out.

They ran over from the windows and wrapped their arms around my mother's waist, yelling out enthusiastic goodbyes and reminding her that we were going on a plane. Then it was my turn. Her face was inscrutable as we embraced briefly. I wanted to say something, but no words came out.

During the flight I felt numb. I tried not to think about my parents driving home from the airport, about my mother trying not to think about us. Twenty-four hours later, when the plane began its final descent into New York, I felt a rush of exhilaration, a familiar feeling from a recurring dream where I'm about to step off a tall building or a cliff, believing almost – but not entirely – that I can fly.

13. Caesar Salad

'YOU'RE GOING TO LOVE THE SALADS in New York.' This had been Martin's constant refrain in the lead-up to our departure. And on our first morning in the Big Apple he was determined to prove it.

My euphoria of the night before was already fading fast as the effects of sleep deprivation took hold. Our hotel, which we'd booked from Australia, had boasted Olde Worlde Charm. The Olde part was right, as evidenced by loud dripping taps, creaky doors and groaning floor joists. Nothing could induce four-year-old Amy to overlook these distractions, place her head on her pillow and *sleep*. Martin, however, was still running on adrenalin and even after a torturous night was ready to show us the sights.

The last thing I felt like on a grey January day was a salad, but after the paltry hotel breakfast I was anxious to get out and see this most exciting of cities, so why not start at a New York salad bar?

Wrapped in our newly acquired coats, gloves, scarves and beanies we ventured out of our Manhattan hotel to hail a cab. To me the idea of hailing a cab epitomised the New York experience, but it turned out to be a competitive business. There we were standing on the sidewalk (as we now called it) hailing away. At length a cab would pull into the kerb and suddenly seven people would appear from nowhere, shouting, and dive in, doors slamming and off they'd go.

Finally we secured our cab, but I was disappointed to find no light-hearted banter from the driver in a Bronx or Brooklyn accent. In fact, I'm not sure he even spoke English (of course he may have thought the same thing about us). The yellow taxis romanticised by Hollywood were just big yellow tanks with slashed seats and no seat-belts. The drivers were insane and hit the horn every ten seconds whether they needed to or not. As we swerved violently between cars I was sure we were going to die, so there seemed little point craning my neck to spot landmarks. But fifteen minutes later we emerged, shaken but unhurt.

'This salad had better be good,' I said, my knees still wobbling.

'Relax,' said Martin. 'Prepare yourself to be impressed.'

A floor to ceiling blackboard listed endless options and combinations of things I'd never heard of – like scallions and cilantro.

'What'll it be?' said the waitress.

'Um …'

'Well?' she snapped her gum.

'What's cilantro?'

'Excuse me?' She rolled her eyes.

I could feel the tension mounting in the line of people behind me.

'I'll just have a chicken Caesar salad.'

'Make that two,' said Martin over my shoulder. 'And two kids-size pasta salads.'

Almost before we reached our table, our order arrived. Mountains of Romaine lettuce and cubed processed chicken in a bowl the size of a Weber lid was slapped down in front of me.

'Enjoy,' said the waitress, devoid of facial expression.

'Didn't I say everything was bigger and better in the States?' said Martin, smugly.

Big tears filled my eyes. I tilted my head up toward the ceiling, determined not to crack in front of the kids. I should have known not to believe Martin, a meat and potatoes man. My heart sank as my panic rose. So this was IT. This was what we'd come all this way for! This is what I'd broken my mother's heart for? I could feel myself surrendering to overwhelming fatigue. Martin and Max both wore 'What the...?' expressions, while Amy toyed distractedly with her pasta, oblivious to my state. It must be jet lag, I told myself.

The thought of spending another night in our creaky hotel room didn't help. Although the container with our furniture was not due to arrive from Australia for six weeks, it was clear that we needed a home of our own right away.

We found a 'realtor' who showed us a house in Montclair, 'a leafy Manhattan commuting suburb' located in New Jersey. And we could move in immediately. 'We'll take it,' we cried.

Of course, our new house would be empty, so it was time for Martin to introduce me to that great American icon – The Mall.

'You can buy absolutely anything, day or night,' he trumpeted.

So we hired a small van and set off for a mega-mall to buy the basics. A TV and VCR were essential, not to mention kitchen appliances, mattresses and bed linen. Martin confidently led the way, unaware that there were numerous entrances to this monolith which all looked identical. We walked in one door in daylight but out another into freezing darkness. Rows of cars stretched out before us, disappearing into the night. We were totally lost and I was scared. People get shot in mall car parks in America. Especially lost people carrying TVs and VCRs. This made the salad episode look good. Frozen solid, we finally stumbled upon the car. So far Martin's PR job was a fizzer and we drove back to the hotel in silence.

The next day we moved out of our squeaky hotel room and into our new home. It was a colonial-style 1920s timber house, quintessentially middle class America. We could have been a TV family as we stood together on the porch to farewell the realtor.

After unpacking our few possessions and setting up mattresses on the bedroom floors, we all collapsed into a dense sleep. When I woke, I was keen to take in my new surroundings. The first thing I noticed was the absence of fences between properties, not even the hedges or shrubbery for privacy that we guard so carefully in Sydney. Our new back yard merged with our neighbour's yard and theirs with their neighbour's. More oddly, there was no sign of life – just vast, empty space with idle swing sets and damp sand pits. The kids were now up, and together we stared out at this wasteland from an upstairs window.

'You said there'd be snowmen,' said Max, a big tear rolling down his cheek.

Yes, I wanted to say, and Fifth Avenue and Central Park and the Empire State Building, but so far we'd seen nothing. The rush of moving had eaten into Martin's few precious free days before he was due to start work. That morning, he had left before daybreak for his first day, so the three of us were on our own.

I had to get Max enrolled in a local school. Armed with the appropriate paperwork, we went to the Board of Education and Max was assigned to a school near our home. We set out the next morning, wrapped in so many layers our arms stuck out sideways, and walked, bent forward at forty-five degrees, straight into the freezing wind. As we rounded the last corner we stopped dead in our tracks. A huge brick edifice rose before us. It appeared to be firmly bolted shut.

'Is that it?' asked Max, his voice shaking.

'I think so.'

A lump formed in my throat. I thought of our cute little primary school back home, its simple, single-storey classrooms and open playground. I gripped the children's hands and marched resolutely towards the steps. The huge double doors were locked but there was an intercom on the wall. I pressed the button.

'Yes?'

I explained who we were and a buzzing noise indicated that we could enter. But I couldn't work out how to open the heavy door in time and it remained locked. Max looked relieved and turned, ready to leave. I pressed the button again. This time when it buzzed I was prepared to wrestle with the door and managed to get in. We followed the signs to the office, and after a brief chat with the principal, a young woman was called to take Max to his classroom. I could see the panic spreading across his face and he had to be peeled from around my waist, tears streaming down his face. I struggled to prevent my own tears from escaping as I wondered what on earth we were doing here.

I realised as he was taken away that I had done very little to prepare him for any cultural differences he may encounter. In fact, the only thing I had mentioned was that Americans avoided using the word 'toilet.' It was considered more polite to say 'bathroom'. He'd looked perplexed.

While he was at school, Amy and I sat on the floor in our upstairs sunroom and played Cloudburst, her favourite game, which I'd squashed into her suitcase. It required four players and involved assembling a house before a roll of the dice caused a rainstorm to ruin your efforts. To make up the foursome it was necessary to recruit a doll and 'Terial' (the important remnants of an old nightie of mine). The long hours stretched out before me as I waited for three o'clock when we could collect Max. There were only so many times that I could endure Cloudburst, which felt more like a description of my state of mind than a child's game.

It took some convincing to get Amy to repeat the arctic walk to school. When Max was finally released he was wearing a wait-till-I-get-you-home expression on his face. Despite my cheery questions, he did not utter a word until we got home. He then made a dive for what is very politely termed 'the powder room' and finally reappeared, red-faced but relieved.

'Oh, Mummy,' he said, 'it was terrible. I've been holding my bathroom all day.'

As the children were eating 'snack' – afternoon tea sounds way too prim in America – Mum rang from Sydney. Max answered the phone and began to sob immediately.

'They don't have rolled oats in America,' he told her. 'I miss eating rolled oats at your house.'

When I finally managed to extricate the phone from his tight little fist, Mum sounded concerned.

'Things must be grim over there if they don't even have rolled oats.'

'I'm sure they have rolled oats,' I said, battling for the second, or was it the third time that day to maintain my composure. I wrote ROLLED OATS on a pad beside the phone.

14. Snowstorm

WHEN NEWS OF THE FIRST SNOWSTORM of the season hit the airwaves there was a buzz of excitement in the air that was palpable. Neighbours from both sides came over to ensure we had snow shovels and advised us to park our car near the street to avoid having to shovel an entire driveway's worth of snow.

Before dawn I was woken by what sounded like a blaring foghorn. I forced myself to consciousness and realised that there was, indeed, a foghorn honking into the darkness. Then I remembered the realtor had mentioned this – it was to announce cancellation of school in snowstorms. This old-fashioned 'town crier' approach seemed incongruous and somehow quaint.

I jumped out of bed and looked out the window. Our garden had been transformed. The branches of trees were heavy with snow. Roads and footpaths had disappeared under a luxurious white blanket, and in the streetlight I could see millions of thick snowflakes still tumbling from the sky.

In the morning, children emerged from surrounding houses to play in the snow. They knocked on our door and invited our kids to join in the construction of an enormous communal snowman.

When school resumed I made sure we arrived in plenty of time. As we approached we were confronted with a sea of colour as beanies, scarves and mittens converged and children poured through the open doors. Funky music blared while the principal, an extremely tall woman, greeted everyone, tapping her ski-like feet to the beat. I could see that Max was impressed with the show.

As Amy and I walked back home, a car pulled up slowly beside us.

'Want a ride? It's too cold for the little one to be walking.'

I looked in the car window and saw a woman about my age behind the wheel. She smiled.

'We live on the same block. I've seen you walking with your kids. I'm Lee.'

It turns out that living on the same block counts for a lot in the States. It means you're practically neighbours, regardless of the length of the block. Lee offered to lend us toys for the children until out container arrived and help get Amy into her son's pre-school. By the time she dropped me home I had decided that as a friend, Lee would be a real catch. It sounded as though her life was already full enough, though. Lee was an artist and had a studio at home. She also taught art at one of the local schools, as well as at the art museum. She lived in a quirky house with curved walls and a bright yellow front door, which she pointed out as we drove past.

I was determined to somehow wheedle my way into her life. I had several things in my favour: we lived on the same block, and it turned out Max was in her daughter's class at school. Soon after this encounter, I acquired a car of my own, and one of the first things I did with my new-found independence was to offer to car-pool with Lee.

We quickly fell into a daily routine with the driving, and the kids became close friends. Lee was kind and wise and, although she didn't know it, I came to rely on her heavily.

Martin's work schedule continued to be torturous, requiring him to work ridiculously long hours. Sometimes we'd barely have a complete conversation all week.

'I didn't think it would be this crazy,' he said one Saturday morning. 'I can see I'm not going to be around much. Why don't you look into doing a course or something?'

It was a good idea, but I had no idea what I wanted to do. My first goal was to get to know the city. Once the kids were settled at school and pre-school, I would head in whenever possible. On each occasion, as the bus approached the Lincoln Tunnel, I was struck by the panoramic view of the New York skyline. From the peak of the Empire State Building at Midtown it fell away towards Lower Manhattan, only to be interrupted by the giant Twin Towers, which totally dwarfed their surroundings. The scene could have been phoney, like a backdrop to a movie – a movie I was now in.

By coincidence, the cousin of a friend of mine lived in Montclair, so we were put in touch with each other. Allison and I hit it off immediately. She had previously been a television news reporter but now wanted to switch to acting. While she waited for a break into that industry, she kept her hand in by doing television commercials. She might have three or four auditions a week in Manhattan, and having grown up there, knew it intimately. Often she asked me to join her on these jaunts. After her audition, we'd end up somewhere interesting – a little hole-in-the-wall café in Tribeca or the viewing of an off-Broadway rehearsal that she somehow knew about. As well as acting, Allison also had an interest in writing. For some reason, she thought I should consider writing too. She suggested the New School for Social Research in Greenwich Village had an extensive writing program.

Although the idea of writing had never occurred to me before, the thought of doing anything in Greenwich Village was irresistible, so I signed up for a short course.

Even from the first exercise we were asked to do, I was completely hooked. Using various themes or stimulus material, we would have to write for three or five or maybe ten minutes without lifting our pens from the page. I'd take these scribbled stories I'd done in class and work on them at home. My handbag was full of bits of paper or envelopes I'd jotted thoughts onto as they popped into my head. In the middle of the night I might have to write down a word or phrase I'd been searching for to complete a story. The real mystery to me was that I'd never thought to do this before.

During my lunch breaks at the New School, I'd explore the surrounding area. I discovered that people from this part of town were not interested in Midtown shops or Central Park. In fact, to them, anything above Twenty-First Street was considered passé. And so I began to learn about the neighbourhoods of Manhattan.

At first I had thought this was just a quirk of the suburbs, but it seems that New Yorkers are extraordinarily attached to their neighbourhoods. There had to be a damn good reason to venture from Eleventh Street up to Midtown.

One good reason, of course, would be to see a show. The half-price ticket booth for Broadway shows provided a great way for us to entertain Martin's clients or visitors from Australia. We'd go in on the PATH train to Hoboken wharf and catch a ferry across the Hudson River to the World Trade Center where the ticket booth was located. The sheer magnitude of the Twin Towers, which loomed overhead as the ferry drew into the wharf, was thrilling beyond words.

After the course at the New School concluded, I took a writing course in Montclair where I met other local writers. We formed a writing group, which included Allison, and although they were more experienced than I was, they were generous in their encouragement. We met monthly and it quickly became the most important date on my calendar.

Since our arrival, phone calls from Mum had been frequent, brief and business-like. Had we updated our health insurance? Would our tax return be submitted on time? Had I located rolled oats in the supermarket? She was frantically busy, she told me. Too busy to write. With echoes of my time in Berlin, I was prevented from elaborating on any details in our life – the children's school, new friends or our wonderful neighbours.

Waiting for our furniture to arrive from Australia, I had mentally rehearsed where I wanted everything to go, but when it was finally all unpacked and put in place I realised there was an empty space – a piano space. No matter how I rearranged the furniture, that space was still there. I ached at the loss all over again.

I was astounded at my own stupidity that I had not just brought it with me. What did my mother know about how well pianos travel? For the second time I was overwhelmed with anger at her – or perhaps it was at myself. Why did she have to make it so hard for me?

I started scanning newspaper advertisements for pianos. I found one that seemed well priced and went to have a look at it.

The owner was an elderly woman with arthritic hands. She took me into a cluttered living room where the piano was nestled in amongst other well-loved pieces. It was a dainty Krakauer spinet with French provincial legs, so different from the heavy upright I'd lost.

'Do you play, dear?' she asked.

'Not really. I just think every home should have one.'

'Yes, I've been trying to get my son to take this one, but he's not interested. I hope he doesn't regret it.'

He will, I thought to myself.

After checking that it was in tune and that all the keys worked, I didn't know what else to look at, so I lifted the top. There it was – an oval, brass plate, decoratively engraved with the words 'New York'. That was it – I had to have it.

When I told Martin that at three hundred dollars the piano was an absolute steal, he looked doubtful. What did I know about buying a piano? How much research had I done? But he came around.

'I suppose it can't be that much of a lemon,' he said. 'You should have lessons while we're here.'

'Maybe the kids could learn, too,' I said.

When the piano was unloaded by the removalists several days later, I hovered like a nervous parent.

'She's a pretty little thing,' one of them said, and I felt absurdly proud. Once it was settled in its corner, I couldn't stop looking at it. I'd walk into the living room just to look at my new piano.

After that I launched myself into other projects. I explored furnishing stores and came home armed with swathes of stripes and florals I never would have considered in Sydney. I felt excited as I unpacked my impulsive purchases. Making curtains for the children's rooms, finishing the sofa cover, even brazenly machine hemming, gave me a rush of independence.

It took me months to tell Mum about the piano, but finally I blurted out the news in a phone call.

'Mum, I've bought a piano.'

'… A piano?'

'Yes, a Krakauer spinet. It's very dainty.'

'I've never heard of it – sounds more like a harpsichord. Are you sure it's a piano?'

'Yes, Mum. I'm going to take lessons.'

'Really?' There was a moment's silence before she continued. 'Well, I suppose those long fingers of yours could be pianist's fingers.'

'You and Dad should come for a visit and you could see it.'

'Yes, but we couldn't leave the garden, and Dad's got so many doctor's appointments. Anyway, why don't you send me a photo of it and I'll show it to our old piano tuner – he'll know what it is.'

'Trust me, Mum, it's a piano.'

15. Cape Cod

THE SEASONS IN NEW YORK change suddenly and dramatically. The interminably long winters hang on until one day you wake up and it's spring. Blue skies and crisp, clear air mark a change in season as well as mood. Almost overnight dogwoods and cherry blossoms burst into bloom. I had always wanted a dogwood in my garden but Mum had said that it was too warm to grow them reliably in Sydney. In Montclair, however, they grew like weeds, their elegant cup-shaped blooms balancing precariously on graceful branches which spread out horizontally from the trunk.

Every weekend the schools held their spring fairs, attended in large numbers by locals, newly energised following the winter thaw. A sense of goodwill seemed to infuse everything. The public gardens were an explosion of colour, where drifts of irises covered the gently sloping field. Children took sketchbooks and crayons or watercolours to capture the scene on paper.

The topic of conversation had switched from when the next snowstorm would hit to discussions of when you were 'putting your garden in'. At first I didn't know what they meant, but at the spring fairs I noticed almost everyone carrying trays of petunias and other annuals back to their car. On weekends garden nurseries were now bursting with people buying endless trays of petunias. I, too, began buying petunias, though I could imagine my mother's horror, not to mention Aunt Alice's, that this 'potted colour' was now the extent of my garden. Petunias were only a garnish. Where was the heart and soul?

I plonked in my petunias, with a simultaneous sense of guilt and liberation that I had no intention of devoting any time to this garden at all. By the time we'd left Sydney, I'd become so preoccupied with gardening that if Max wanted to wind me up, he'd threaten to run out and jump on my cuttings. It had also become a trigger point for arguments between Martin and me. His idea of a Saturday morning was to sit on the front verandah with a cup of coffee and the newspaper. To me this was wasting precious moments that should be spent weeding or mowing or pruning or doing *something* constructive in the garden. On one such Saturday morning in Sydney, a friend dropped in to find Martin with his coffee and paper while I was out at a nursery picking up mulch. She told me later how much she envied my husband's European sophistication, complaining that her husband was forever putting in ag-pipes or building retaining walls. I wondered who should be envying whom.

'We work all week,' Martin would say. 'Weekends are for relaxing, not labouring.'

I couldn't really argue with that. Well, I tried, but there was no denying he had a valid point. Martin had once been a keen golfer. As he pointed out, he no longer played because it took up too much family time. He didn't fancy gardening as a substitute. A few years of no gardening altercations might not be a bad thing. So in went the petunias, but when I stepped back to admire the results I was not impressed. This previously snow-covered garden bed was going to need a lot more than a few trays of petunias to improve it.

As summer approached, massive booklets came home from school advertising the plethora of options for summer camp. They were mostly all-day affairs packed with action and adventure. I couldn't imagine my kids being rapt in the idea. They both loved hanging out and creating their own imaginary games – and there were plenty of possibilities in our own back yard. We had a stream running through the property and our garage, which was nestled in among trees, had a loft-cubby with windows overlooking the stream. We now also had a cat – a beautiful fellow called Winston. A family nearby was moving to an apartment and everything had to go. Lee agreed to take their bird and dog. Other neighbours helped themselves to furniture. Max, Amy and I looked on from the sidewalk.

'Can we take something, too?' asked Max.

Before I could respond, the owner approached us carrying a very mellow-looking Abyssinian cat. 'Your kids look the right age for this guy. He's a beautiful boy. Eight years old. He'd slot right in. Here, hold him.'

Winston, a huge cat, melted into my arms. As far as sales tactics go it was as effective as it was ruthless. Max and Amy practically leapt on him, stroking his fur and begging for a turn to hold him. They were desperate for a pet but it had never been the right time. Now was almost certainly not the right time, but poor Winston clearly had to go somewhere. We took him home. He certainly was the most relaxed cat I'd ever met. Amy carried him around for the entire afternoon, his feet almost dragging on the floor, and Max had plans to have sleepovers with him in the cubby.

This time Martin really did think I'd flipped.

'What are we going to do with a cat when we go back to Australia?'

'He's already eight – we're here for four years. How long do they live?' I said, in a lame attempt at obfuscation.

'You're asking *me* how long cats live?'

I changed tack. 'It will be good for the kids to learn responsibility and he'll be good company for them over the summer. You won't even know he's here.'

He could see it was a done deal. 'He'd better not lie on my jacket. Ever!'

We were all hankering for a family holiday but the pressure of Martin's job still had not eased up. There was no chance of him taking time for a vacation and his absence highlighted the fact that we had no family nearby. In a happy coincidence, my brother Tim had moved to Boston the year before our move. Although Boston was four to five hours away, compared to Australia it felt close so when we needed a family fix we would visit for the weekend. As an adult Tim had lost his lisp and was fantastic with the kids, something I could never have anticipated from the Evans Head days. I told myself we'd be fine with the cubby, the cat and the trip to Boston, and surely not *everyone* we knew would leave town.

With all this time on our hands, I looked into piano lessons. I contacted a woman from an ad in the local paper who would come to the house. She thought Amy was a bit young, but perhaps Max, now aged six, would be interested if I had a lesson as well. The two children watched on for a short while but quickly lost interest. Max announced that he was not the piano type, but I persevered with my lessons with painfully slow progress.

'When are you going to play a grown-up's song?' shouted Max one day over my rendition of *Row Your Boat*. Not any time soon, I didn't think. The only one who appreciated my musical endeavours was Winston, who came running in to sit with me and purr loudly as soon as he heard me play a note. I just wished I had more to work with than children's songs.

Then the summer hit with a ferocity that I had not expected. The heat and humidity rivalled anything I'd experienced back home, but without the southerly buster or sea breeze to cool things off. We were landlocked, and Montclair was empty. Everyone we knew *did* leave town, or their kids were away or at camp. The loft was now a hot, sticky haven for wasps and the stream was a mosquito breeding ground. Max, Amy and I sat in the kitchen with the air-conditioner labouring under the strain, while Winston dozed on a sunny windowsill. I wondered how on earth we'd fill two months.

During those interminable weeks, I became aware of a tingling over my right eye that came and went. At first it was almost imperceptible, like a shadow passing over my face. I ignored it, as you do a muscle twitch or unexplained knee pain. Then the frequency and intensity increased and began to move down my face, until it hovered over the right side of my lip. At times my tongue felt thick, almost clumsy, and I thought I sounded drunk. Martin said he couldn't hear any difference in my speech but I went to see a neurologist. Like Martin, he was not overly impressed with my symptoms but ordered a brain scan anyway and said he'd ring with the results.

I tried to put it out of my mind and distracted myself by searching the internet for short getaway trips and came up with a solution at Cape Cod. I managed to cajole Martin into taking a couple of days off and we packed up the car and left on a Friday night.

After an excruciating drive into Cape Cod (as the entire North East population had apparently had the same idea) we arrived at our hotel room, which overlooked the bay and breakwater. Martin took the kids down to the beach and I went for a walk along the breakwater. That's where I was when the doctor rang.

'There is no tumour,' he had said in a tone that told me the kicker was still to come. 'But the scan shows several small white dots. It could be multiple sclerosis.'

I felt momentarily disorientated, almost dizzy. Despite the episode in Germany when those words were first mentioned, I had somehow managed to completely avoid considering this as a possibility. My mind went simultaneously into overdrive and shutdown. I struggled to process those two words: multiple sclerosis. I tried to remember what the textbooks had said, to bring patients to mind who did not have paralysed limbs and incontinence bags. I tried hard not to think about Venus.

'This doesn't have to be bad news, does it?' I asked stupidly.

'Well, it's not good news. This is your brain we're talking about. When you get back we'll do more investigations to confirm the diagnosis.' And that was it.

I dropped the phone into my pocket and stared out over the bay. Everything had gone quiet. I walked along the breakwater and then looked back towards the beach. Martin was playing with the kids at the water's edge. They all waved to me, but their movements were in slow motion. Their mouths were moving but no sound came out. They looked like marionettes. I waved back mechanically and kept walking.

'We don't know anything yet,' said Martin when I managed to pull him aside to tell him. 'It mightn't be MS at all. Let's just wait to see what the other tests show.'

But I didn't need to wait for the tests. Somewhere in the recesses of my brain I'd been waiting for this to catch up with me for over a decade. I just had a sick feeling in the pit of my stomach. This was always going to happen.

'We don't know anything yet,' Martin repeated. He tried to look reassuring.

I nodded, but I couldn't bring myself to respond.

Our few days on Cape Cod were strained. Martin and I could only talk when the kids were occupied with sandcastles or swimming. Our brief snatches of conversation were inevitably interrupted and we'd flip back into upbeat-parent mode until we could steal another few moments of privacy. It was a strange limbo land we'd found ourselves in. I'd sit with the kids, absently loading fistfuls of sand onto yet another castle, and ponder the way the breakwater stretched endlessly into the vast expanse of the bay, like an endless arrow pointing to nowhere. What was its function? In the evenings it disappeared beneath thick fog, which shrouded the peninsula in its weighty, humid air.

I didn't know what to do with myself. I felt agitated, like someone who has given up smoking and needs something to do with their hands. I bought a notebook and began to write an oddly detached story, not about me, but about some other young woman, a loner, afflicted by strange neurological symptoms. When I felt the pressure building up inside me, I wrote. It was like releasing a valve, allowing me to return to my usual role, unencumbered, for a while. When the pressure built up again, I'd pull out the notebook and add to my pages. And so, I established a routine that saw me through those early, weird days.

When we returned to Montclair, I went through the motions of having the diagnosis confirmed: blood tests, more blood tests and finally a lumbar puncture.

'It appears that you have indeed had an episode of multiple sclerosis.' The neurologist delivered his verdict impassively.

Martin and I sat there in his plush Upper West Side office, our hands folded in our laps like well-behaved school children, hoping to impress the principal. We waited for him to elaborate but he didn't.

'What does this mean?' asked Martin finally. 'What can we expect?'

'It's impossible to tell. It's a degenerative neurological condition where the patient's immune system attacks the myelin sheaths surrounding the nerves. This interrupts the transmission of electrical impulses to and from the brain. Scar tissue forms at the site of an attack, which shows up on the MRI as white spots. These spots or plaques are what we saw on your wife's brain scan. The more plaques, generally the greater the level of disability.'

So far he'd given me nothing useful. This much I already knew. At the same time, I was sure Martin wouldn't have understood a word.

I told him about the weird experience I'd had of losing my sense of taste in Germany twelve years earlier. He agreed that in the light of the present diagnosis, it was no doubt an early episode of MS.

'It's a long time between episodes, though. You may turn out to have a relatively benign course of the disease,' he said.

He described the different stages of MS. To begin with it is usual to have the so-called relapsing/remitting variety, in which there is full or almost full recovery after each episode. However, most people eventually go on to develop the more progressive form, where there is limited recovery after each attack so the amount of disability is accumulated. He told us about a new treatment for MS requiring regular injections that modify the immune system, reducing the number of attacks, but he didn't think that was necessary yet. In any case, I wasn't eligible because to qualify there needed to be three confirmed episodes. I wasn't sure if that was the good news or the bad news.

'What about diet?' asked Martin 'There must be something we can do there?'

'There's a thing called the Swank diet but it's very complicated and there's no evidence it helps. It's up to you,' he said and stood up, indicating the consultation was over.

As we headed for the elevator Martin tried to sound positive.

'Maybe the Swank diet would help,' he said. But he looked more shaken than I'd ever seen him.

'Shouldn't we ring your parents?' he asked.

'No, definitely not.' I was surprised by my own response. 'I've got to work it out myself.'

Against my better judgment, I perused the internet. Lists of frightening symptoms would appear on the screen and I'd feel my throat constrict with fear as my future was laid out before me. Or I might stumble upon the promise of a miracle cure in a bottle for $59.95, followed by pages of testimonials from satisfied customers. The curious thing was that after each roller coaster ride on the internet, I'd log off and, like Alice stepping back through the looking glass, I'd find myself safely in my study where nothing had changed. I could still walk and talk; I was still me.

I gave up on the strange world of cyberspace and requested some printed material from the MS Association. Whenever I was struck by a wave of panic, I'd distract myself by working on my peculiar short story. Perhaps it was that sense I'd always had of being an outsider looking in on life that allowed me to observe my protagonist from a distance. Often in those pre-dawn hours when sleep eluded me, I contemplated not my own future, but whether or not to allow her to survive.

So far only Martin knew of my diagnosis, but something made me mention it to Lee one afternoon.

She absorbed the news in her quiet, inimitable way, her tiny frame dwarfed by the huge Adirondack chair she was sitting in.

'You know what?' she said, 'It seems to me that it's the creative people who get multiple sclerosis.'

There were plenty of creative people in my family who could draw or paint, but I was not one of them. It had always been a source of frustration to me that I'd been overlooked when those genes were dished out.

'I'm not creative,' I said.

'Sure you're creative. It's something to do with the way you see the world. Anyway, I can tell from your eyes – the way the light bounces off your eyes – it's like they have a lot of surfaces.'

I had no idea what, if anything, eyes and light reflection had to do with being creative, but because Lee was wise, I believed her. I felt chuffed. Wow, I was creative! Only creative people get MS. So, if I had to have MS in order to be creative, that was fine – as long as I never got sick.

Over the next month the tingling in my face resolved and I felt as though the error had been rectified. I was not a patient – there was nothing wrong with me.

In the autumn I signed up for another writing course at the New School.

16. Twilight Zone

WHEN MARTIN TOLD ME he'd been recalled to the office in Sydney earlier than originally planned, I felt as if I'd been slapped, leaving a hot sting that spread across my face.

'But what about the four years?' I said.

'Well, it turns out to be more like three.'

'But I'm not ready!' Even as the words came out, I knew how naïve they sounded.

'These things happen in big companies,' said Martin. 'They move people around.'

I felt utterly powerless. So completely had I immersed myself in my new life that the prospect of leaving it was unimaginable. It wasn't that I didn't want to return to Sydney – just not yet. I wasn't *finished* here yet. What about my writing course? What about my writing group? What about MS? In that instant, I realised how much had changed for me since we arrived here.

My brain refused to accept that soon our existence here would be just a memory. New people would move into our house, cook in our kitchen and be embraced by our neighbourly neighbourhood.

It's a strange sort of twilight zone existence when you know things are about to change irreversibly in the near future, but in the meantime, you have to attend to the daily business of living. The children still had to go to school, the shopping still needed to be done, clothes had to be washed and Winston needed to be fed, little suspecting that his life, too, was about to change. We had all fallen for Winston. Even Martin's cat-hardened heart had softened, but I had fallen the hardest. Still, the sadness I felt at the thought of leaving him was disproportionate, as though I were leaving my first-born child.

I put an ad in the local paper to find a new owner for him: 'Eleven-year-old de-sexed male Abyssinian, free to good home.' I thought it would be difficult to place such an old cat, but my advertisement drew all the psycho-Abyssinian lovers out of the closet, begging to take Winston. I told Martin there was no way I was handing him over to such zealots.

Martin was too nice to give me the 'I told you so' routine about the dangers of getting a cat when you're living in a foreign country. And clearly he thought I was a bit of a psycho-Abyssinian zealot, myself, but none of that helped me now.

When you're faced with something almost too big to absorb, the pain can be distilled down into one or two images. In this case, Winston came to symbolise everything I was about to leave behind. I might be absent-mindedly packing or sorting, and he'd rub past my leg or put his paws around my neck when I picked him up, and without warning, tears would spring into my eyes. I'd quickly pull myself together before the kids spotted me, berating myself for such self-indulgence. After all, people moved all the time. I should just be grateful to have had the opportunity of living here. And Sydney was my home. However, no amount of self-talk could dispel the overpowering sensation that I was looking into a void.

It had taken me a full week after receiving the news before I could bring myself to tell Lee. I had this irrational sense that for as long as the words remained unspoken, I could forestall the reality. But one afternoon as I was dropping her kids home, I forced myself to mention it.

'It had to happen sooner or later,' I said light-heartedly. 'I guess it's for the best, before the kids get too much older.'

I couldn't meet her gaze and reversed out of the driveway before she could respond.

The following weeks became filled with activity. I had to organise removalists, and tear into Manhattan for a last look at museums or the last opportunity to buy from a New York department store. One afternoon, Lee rang me and I greeted her in my usual upbeat manner, but she interrupted me.

'Libby, we have to talk about this,' she said.

That's all it took. My throat constricted and I couldn't speak. Tears poured down my cheeks, flooded down, like Niagara Falls.

'Libby?'

I tried to squeak a response so she'd know I was still there, but nothing came out.

'I'm coming over,' she said.

A few minutes later we were sitting together in my kitchen. I still couldn't say anything very coherent and Lee didn't need to say much. She was just there.

Perhaps in an attempt to completely suspend reality I booked three days for us in Disneyland on our way home. For the children this was enough to mitigate any doubts they had about our big move. Ever since I was a child I'd had a very clear picture of what Disneyland would be like: a fantasy kingdom set in a magical land. However, it turned out that Disneyland is located on the edge of the biggest parking lot I had ever seen in my life, which itself is plonked in the heart of an urban sprawl which extends from Mexico to Oregon.

We checked into the hotel room that afforded us an uninterrupted view of the massive car park, miniaturised from our seventh floor window. Cars and buses stretched back to the horizon, all agitating to get to the front of the queue. But here in Disneyland's car park, America's extraordinary organisational skills came to the fore. Once through the gates vehicles fell into orderly lines and, as if by magic, were deposited neatly into their allocated spot. Tourist buses spewed forth their cargo, tiny people who scurried towards the entrance gates, where once again, order reigned in the form of a neat queue.

We left our hotel room to join that queue. Relentlessly cheerful staff were ready to calm frayed nerves to facilitate our smooth transition into the other dimension.

Martin took charge of the map and directed us towards the gentler rides, but it didn't take long for Max and Amy to work out that there were more exciting things on offer. They ran from one attraction to another, not in the least deterred by the length of queues and if Minnie or Mickey walked by it was a real brush with fame. Sometimes I'd take a break, sitting on a bench in the sunshine while Martin took them on a ride. Here in this strange land I felt disconnected from the past and the future, as though we might remain suspended in this moment forever.

As darkness fell, we headed for the exit. Set against a dusky-pink sky was the Disneyland Castle, playing its nostalgic theme song. I was transported to the Sunday evenings of my childhood with melted cheese on toast, watching Disneyland on TV. The song marked the end of the show, as well as the end of the weekend, causing a sudden pit to form in my stomach at the thought of school the next day. I would remember an assignment or homework I was meant to have completed. As I canvassed excuses, the song would continue in the background.

'When you wish upon a star your dreams coooome truuuue ...'

These optimistic words set inexplicably in a mournful minor key just deepened my sense of foreboding.

17. Marzipan (ii)

FOR YEARS MUM HAD TALKED about writing a book that classifies plants into gingham, linen or silk. 'A garden only needs these three,' she'd say. Any plant which could not be so classified should be consigned to the compost heap. The friendly faces of shasta daisies, for example, are gingham, while the beauty of an old fashioned rose is pure silk.

Now that I was home, Mum was aching to take me around all her favourite nurseries – none of the big commercial ones, of course, but her specially selected boutique nurseries.

'You'll really have to get stuck into that garden of yours,' she said. 'It hasn't had much attention since you left. Of course, you can't expect tenants to tend a garden.'

I knew my days of filling up space with trays of petunias were over. Three years' worth of neglect might as well have been a lifetime, but I was unable to muster the enthusiasm to get in there and tackle it.

My sense of dislocation was consolidated by the searing November heat juxtaposed with bearded Santas and fake snow on shop windows. Naturally, Mum never asked about my time overseas, about the people I'd met or the life I'd led. She didn't ask if I was glad to be back. It was as though the whole aberration had never happened. And in a sense, it was easier that way.

Dad was more interested – or at least tried to be. He was curious about traffic jams and crime in Manhattan. Or if I mentioned that one of my friends was an artist he'd want to know everything about the work she did. But several days later we'd go over the same things again. Dad had always been like this – every good intention of being involved but never quite able to retain the pertinent details. Perhaps now, though, it was more marked.

Still, they were both overjoyed to have the children back. Dad got a kick out of their American accents and kept asking them to say certain words. And Max and Amy were equally delighted to have their grandparents around the corner, and uncles, aunts and cousin not far away. Kids seem to live in the moment, so they either didn't notice or didn't care that there was little reference from Mum to our life overseas.

I forced myself to go through the motions of preparing the family for a festive Christmas but my heart wasn't in it. Neither was my mind or my body. I looked and felt dreadful. I missed my cat. I missed my friends. I sent them cheery emails and told them of our progress, but it didn't change the fact that I was a very long way away. And I was so incredibly tired.

On Christmas Eve Martin gave me a box of marzipan chocolates as he did every Christmas. I didn't want to open it; I already knew something was wrong. It had been creeping up on me for a few days – a repeat performance of that first MS episode in Berlin. I'd have thought the memory of those symptoms might have faded in the intervening twelve years, but it came flooding back: the bizarre sense that I was tasting something dead, the enormous effort required to overcome the paralysed muscles on one side of my throat. I felt as if I'd been stalked by this MS predator that had been lurking, ready to pounce at the worst possible moment. Why did it have to be now?

When I told Martin it was back, he looked shocked. I realised that he, too, had managed to convince himself it would never happen again.

'Should we go to the hospital?' he said.

'On Christmas Eve? I don't think so. Please just don't mention it to anyone.'

Lunch the next day was held at my parents' house accompanied by the usual Christmas Day commotion. I knew no one would notice if I didn't eat much. As with the previous episode, if I took small mouthfuls and kept the food to the left side, I could swallow it.

The days between Christmas and New Year were spent finding a neurologist who would see me. He ordered a brain scan and asked us to come in for the results on New Year's Eve. It wasn't really necessary – I knew what it would reveal. Martin asked him what we could expect now. His answer was the same as that of his New York counterpart. No one knew. We asked about the injections but he did not think they were justified. However, he conceded that he was 'old school' and was yet to be convinced of the merit of such expensive treatment.

For the first time since my diagnosis I was really angry with the world. I was angry with Martin's company for moving us back here early. If I were still there, still with my writing group or having a coffee with Lee, this would never have happened. I wanted to turn back the clock and stall time so we never reached this moment. But I didn't mention it to anyone. Not even Lee. I didn't think I could find the words over the phone. As with the previous episodes, it took about a month for the symptoms to subside. But I no longer had the ability to put it out of my mind.

Natasha and Meredith both knew of the very early experience I'd had in Berlin all those years ago, and that the outside possibility of MS had been raised. They also sensed that things had not been right with me since I'd been home. It was time to have a conversation with them. Both took the news quietly and undramatically, offering support. I insisted I was managing well and only needed their secrecy. I was still not ready to tell my family.

I did my best to slot back into Sydney life where I'd left off but somehow the slot was now a different shape – or maybe it was me. I had that oddly familiar sense of being an outsider – but now I found it disconcerting – I was *meant* to belong here. When a former colleague rang to offer me a part-time job in her new private practice, I took it. I didn't know how I'd find the energy but I hoped a bit of structure in my life would help.

One afternoon when I was collecting the kids from school, a friend mentioned she had found a wonderful piano teacher. My lessons in Montclair had been uninspiring and had petered out but Amy seemed to be quite musical and now, aged seven, might benefit.

Beata was a strongly built Czech woman with a broad face and intelligent eyes. Amy took to her immediately and although she struggled to crack the code of reading music, Beata's creative approach to teaching made it fun. She would line up pieces of string on the floor like a stave and pretend to be the notes. 'A' was for Amy, she lived in the middle space. 'B' was for Beata, she lived on the middle line. She made the notes come alive. Amy hugged her at the end of each lesson.

Beata asked me if I played and I told her of my failed attempts.

'What would you like to play?' she said.

'I don't know – good stuff, fun stuff. Things I can sing to. I'm too old to go back to basics.'

She pulled out several books of sheet music.

'How about some of these?'

I leafed through the books. Elton John, Andrew Lloyd Webber, Beethoven.

'I don't think I could handle these yet,' I said.

'Yes you could, Libby. I will help you.'

Beata was quiet and encouraging and was able to teach me to play things far beyond my ability. Bit by bit we'd put a piece together, her sturdy fingers taking the base part when I couldn't manage.

On my days off when the kids were at school, I practised as if for an important concert. Apart from emails to my friends in Montclair, I hadn't written a word since my return to Sydney. There was nothing I wanted to say. Nothing I even wanted to think about. Instead, I practised the piano.

18. Idiots and Icons

PEOPLE SAY THAT IN DIFFICULT TIMES, when a family most needs to pull together, they are least able to do so. Mum and I are like that. We don't function well together in difficult times.

I don't know if that's because we're too much alike or too different.

When Mum first noticed the deterioration in Dad, my brothers and I didn't take it too seriously. Although I'd noticed a slight difference in the six months since we'd been home, he'd always been vague. Then all of a sudden, it hit us. In a matter of weeks he descended into a fugue of confusion and disorientation, and became so overwhelmed by fatigue that on some days he was almost unrousable. He barely ate, and had lost his sense of balance. He was disappearing before our eyes.

The GP gave us referrals to take him to various doctors: a geriatric specialist, a vascular physician, and a neurologist – the same one I'd seen at Christmas. I was worried he'd mention my MS in front of Mum, but he showed no hint of recognition.

It required two people to get Dad to these appointments so my brothers and I took it in turns to help Mum. He had brain scans, blood tests, even a psychiatric assessment in case he was depressed. Still, he continued to deteriorate. The diagnosis was vascular dementia, a progressive deterioration of the blood vessels of the brain – there was no treatment.

Matthew was the most involved as he was living with my parents at the time. In the middle of the night – often more than once – he and Mum would have to lift Dad up from the floor after he'd collapse while trying to find the bathroom. During the day, care fell on Mum's shoulders with me attempting to provide backup. I'd try to encourage him to eat something – slivers of mango or avocado, yoghurt, anything at all – but he had no appetite. A community worker called in and provided Mum with brochures with grand mission statements, but the promises of community support never materialised. My offers of help appeared inadequate, a naïve offering in the face of such a crisis.

'Why don't you have a break and go back to playing bridge now?' I asked once we had a routine of sorts.

'How can I? You know I can't just leave Dad, and you get too busy on your day off.'

'But tell me in advance. Let's make a plan.'

'Anyway, I don't feel like playing bridge at the moment.' End of story.

I became edgy during these conversations; I was always on the defensive.

Eventually, Dad became so weak and dehydrated that he had to be hospitalised. As he was carried out of his beloved home on a stretcher to the waiting ambulance, we knew he wouldn't be back. But still I couldn't find the right words for Mum.

The social worker at the hospital found a nursing home for him – a grey, depressing institution. The faint smell of urine hung in the air, and sad, old people were parked in various corners, left to slide out of their wheelchairs. However, this subject was also a no-go zone. It was impossible to raise the possibility of moving Dad because Mum feared that another nursing home might be worse. Maybe she was right, but I was boiling over with frustration that my opinion was of no consequence. I felt locked out.

Mum was now engaged in a daily battle with nursing staff to ensure basic levels of care were provided for Dad. She railed against the staff's lack of care and understanding of someone with dementia. She railed against their lack of compassion. She railed against anyone who disagreed with her. When she was not taking on the Aged Care system single-handedly, she sat beside Dad and knitted. Hour after hour she knitted in his narrow room overlooking the Pacific Highway as trucks zoomed past, their diesel fumes wafting in through the window.

Even before Dad became ill, he had grown increasingly dependent on Mum. He'd had to give up his driver's licence after scraping the car on pillars in public car parks on numerous occasions, ultimately having a minor collision with another car. He had arrived home furious after the prang.

'Her number plate was H-A-G. HAG!' he had said, his jaw set firm. 'How appropriate!'

'But, Dad, you did back into her car.'

'Yes, but how was I to know she was going to just materialise from nowhere like that?'

Mum had his eyes checked. There were pinpoint blind spots, possibly caused by tiny blocked blood vessels – he shouldn't have been driving. So after that Mum drove him everywhere.

She encouraged him to take up art and he re-discovered his love of painting. The class was held at the local scout hall and sometimes I'd collect him if Mum was busy. On one occasion I remember him sitting on a fold-up chair outside the hall, waiting for me to arrive. An easel and sketchbook leaned against the chair. Looking up, he gave me one of his ambiguous smiles and I wondered what he was thinking.

'Sorry I'm late,' I said as I walked around to open the car door for him.

It was always a shock to see the little sparrow legs that stuck out below his trousers when he was sitting down. His hair was thinning and his eyes were almost too big, but somehow he retained a certain look – maybe Basil Rathbone meets John Cleese.

He painstakingly lowered himself into the front seat of my car, his over-sized sketchbook getting stuck in the doorframe.

'How was the class?'

He launched into a blow-by-blow description of that day's lesson and the art teacher's near genius ability. As we turned into his driveway he opened the sketchbook on his lap to show me the day's efforts. I glanced at the work that he was describing in great detail. I was impressed – I couldn't draw to save my life – but I was in a hurry.

'Have you got a minute to come inside and see a few I did last week?'

I made my excuses as I unloaded the chair and easel from the boot and carried them up the sandstone path to the front door. I watched him inch his way up the uneven path, his big plodding shoes dropping heavily to the ground with each step. He caught my eye.

'Silly old bugger,' he said.

He was meant to walk every day to keep the blood circulating to his feet, but even in his special shoes it was too painful.

As a younger man he'd painted, though not often. From time to time, he'd work on his self-portrait, exaggerating the bump on his nose and the slight asymmetry of his mouth caused by Bell's palsy. Dad had contracted the virus in New Guinea almost as soon as he'd arrived to fight in the dying moments of the war. His heroes were Weary Dunlop and Douglas Bader, and he'd been determined that he, too, would make a contribution to the war effort. But as it turned out, his tour of duty was spent in an army base hospital, forced to listen to the exploits of those who had seen action. The ironic expression of Dad's caricature on canvas told the story.

He could have been a cartoonist. He was constantly doodling on notepads, envelopes – any scrap of paper he could find. Effortlessly, almost subconsciously, his hand would fly across the page and a scene would appear, capturing an absurd moment in an otherwise ordinary day. Once he whipped up a giant cartoon of Rolf Harris on the back of a door he was meant to be staining. Rolf's head with beard, big glasses and pointy chin, so instantly recognisable, was placed on the body of a little kangaroo. He'd done it with a four-inch industrial paint brush – like the one Rolf had used on his TV shows. But instead of cartooning for a living, Dad became the world's most unlikely real estate agent.

Early in his career everything appeared to be as it should. Dad would set off to work looking every bit the young executive. His name on the office door in smart black lettering and the brown Holden parked outside promised a bright future. But in reality, it was always an uncomfortable fit.

Dad could never abide snobbery or suburbia, and selling houses on Sydney's North Shore provided both in abundance. After work he would vent his frustration by impersonating those snobby, suburban matrons he dealt with every day. Eventually they all merged into one infuriating character he named Mrs McGillicutty. The world according to Dad was divided into two groups: Idiots (all the Mrs McGillicuttys) and Icons (war heroes and art teachers). Contemplating either group could move him to equal, though opposite, extremes of passion.

Dad seemed to get old, or at least weighed down early, but the years did nothing to blunt his singular view on life. As entertaining as this always was, when I was short of time, I was careful not to get him started.

I made him a cup of tea and he settled into a chair in a sunny corner of the lounge room. 'I'll have to be carried out of here feet first,' he said. This, too, was a familiar theme. There would be no nursing home for Dad. No, sir. 'When the time comes, just knock me over the head and put me out with the bins on a Thursday night.'

I told him again that I had to go. He nodded and I felt momentarily guilty for resenting this intrusion into my day.

It had already started, of course, the silent invasion of his brain by vascular dementia. But even as the symptoms progressed, Dad remained unaware and unconcerned. No longer inhibited by societal constraints, his sarcastic wit went completely unchecked as all the Mrs McGillicuttys of his past competed to be performed.

In spite of our angst, we laughed. He was the same Dad but more so – a one-man show. But I was reminded of our old lemon tree that bore fruit most prolifically in its final months, or the pear tree in his garden that threw its greatest splash of colour as it prepared to drop its leaves.

When he was inevitably carried out of his house feet-first – though not in the way he'd planned – he was taken to hospital where he was fed with a tube to make him well enough to be placed in a nursing home to die. Mercifully, the futility of this was lost on Dad, but the thing he had always feared most became our reality.

His memory was now all but gone. It was a strain to make conversation with someone who had no present and very little past. He always recognised me but seemed uncomfortable after a few minutes, as if aware that he was unable to keep up his end of the dialogue. So he would turn the conversation to Mum. 'When's Mum coming?' Soon, I'd say, and he was content.

Most of the time he slept, but occasionally there were flashes of his old self as he was faced with the stupidity of people around him. One day I arrived as the meal trays were being cleared away. All his meals were pureed and could not have looked or smelled less appetising.

'So, did we enjoy our lunch today, John?' shouted the dietician in that voice reserved for foreigners or old people.

'Well, I enjoyed mine,' said Dad, one eyebrow raised, 'but I didn't know you'd had any.' He gave me a look, indicating that she must be from the Idiot group. Those were the moments I held onto.

19. A Send-off of Sorts

SEVERAL MONTHS BEFORE DAD went into the nursing home, Martin learned that his father had cancer. It's a common story to be dealing with health issues of aging parents on both sides of the family, but that doesn't make it any easier. Martin immediately flew to Hamburg so he and his sister, Dörte, could travel together to Foehr, the island where their parents still lived. Erich was an independent character and put on a brave face, insisting he was managing perfectly well. Martin stayed for ten days and he and Dörte made a plan for their father's care. The load would fall on Dörte, who would be able to visit on weekends from Hamburg. It weighed heavily on Martin that he was so far away. He spoke to his sister frequently but he felt the distance acutely.

Over the next five months, Erich's condition deteriorated and Martin made two more trips, the last time remaining for a month. Erich had begged Martin not to bring the grandchildren with him for that last visit. He did not want them to see him so ill, something I could understand. Martin and Dörte nursed their father at home until the end. Martin called me in the middle of the night to let me know Erich was gone. I looked at the clock and noted that on Sydney time, it was now the early hours of Max's birthday. That pleased Martin. It somehow closed the circle between the generations.

When Martin arrived back in Sydney he looked somehow altered. At a café by the beach we sat together for many hours as he recounted every detail. The experience had been harrowing; it had also been rewarding. He spoke of the uninterrupted hours he'd had with his father, and of the incredible community support available on this tiny island. Even the undertaker went above and beyond the call of duty. He ran a sort of Steptoe and Son side-operation, a trucking service for home contents, which dovetailed nicely into his funeral business. Martin and I ended up laughing until the tears ran down our cheeks as he recounted Bertrand checking out Erich's furniture and then making a job-lot offer, indicating he was robbing himself to do it for so little.

The year was drawing to a close and we'd been invited to a New Year's Eve party to mark the so-called end of the Millennium. It felt strange and wonderful to be with friends as we moved into a new century. At midnight fireworks exploded and we raised our glasses.

'To no more dramas!' said Martin.

'To no more dramas,' I replied, tapping my champagne glass against his.

That was tempting fate too much. Three weeks later, we were woken by the piercing ring of the telephone. Martin answered it but seemed at a loss to understand what his sister was trying to tell him: their mother, Helga, had died in her sleep. We got up and sat in the kitchen. Martin was too shocked to speak so we just sat there together until it was light.

Helga had shown remarkable fortitude throughout Erich's illness, although she must have been terrified, having never done anything without him. For the last few months of his illness, Erich had moved from the main house to an apartment they owned nearby to take the pressure off Helga, but she had still seen him daily. She had been only days away from moving to a retirement village in Hamburg where she would have been closer to Dörte. But without Erich, it was perhaps a blessing that she never had to make the move.

In the morning Martin booked a flight to Germany. We briefly considered whether we should go together, but decided not to drag the children all that way in the depths of a northern winter. Still, I felt terrible knowing that Martin was facing it alone.

On his return ten days later, he again had tales to tell. Immediately after arriving on the island, a wild storm had hit the North Sea. Trees were uprooted, roads were blocked and the ferries from the mainland were cancelled. Apart from Dörte, who was already there, none of their friends or relatives could get there. So in a small Lutheran church, whipped by roaring winds outside, a tiny funeral was conducted for Helga.

It took Martin some months to find his equilibrium after that. It didn't help that we were in the middle of renovating our house, which was stress-inducing in a whole different way, but the work was essential, so I was happy to take on the responsibility for that.

After my rocky re-entry into life in Sydney, things had settled down for me. My health had gradually improved and I was working part time as an occupational therapist. I'd also begun writing for health and parenting magazines. Max and Amy were both content in school and life gradually returned to a predictable rhythm.

The only thing I struggled with was maintaining any kind of fitness. Some of the women I'd met through the school invited me to join their hit-and-giggle tennis group. That sounded non-threatening so I agreed. The strange thing was that I'd arrive feeling fine and after about twenty minutes would become weak and shaky, as though I was coming down with something. At home, I'd wait to be clobbered by the flu but nothing eventuated. It happened every time, so (choosing not to over think it) I stopped playing.

At the end of that year Martin wanted us all to make the trip to Germany. There were still matters to be finalised and he wanted us to spend Christmas with his sister. Although Max and Amy hadn't seen their grandparents often, our visits had been such happy occasions and Erich, in particular, had been such a devoted grandfather their sense of loss had been acute.

We spent the first week in Martin's home town of Hamburg, catching up with relatives and introducing the kids to cousins they hadn't met before. Then we took a ferry to the island where Helga and Erich had spent the last fifteen years of their lives. Standing on the deck we were whipped by freezing winds as we approached the small fishing village.

I knew the thought of going to his parents' house to sort through a lifetime of possessions was weighing heavily on Martin. After breakfast the next morning, when it was still dark outside, we pulled on coats, gloves and boots and drove the short distance from our apartment to the house.

We spent hours sorting and packing things into boxes, Martin pausing over many items that evoked memories from earlier years. Some things bore a blue sticker that Helga had apparently marked to take with her to the retirement village. Mostly they were of no monetary value – a small dish or a china bird, which made the selection all the more poignant. It was a difficult day and we returned to the apartment exhausted.

After dinner, the phone rang. Martin answered it, then spoke in English, so the caller was clearly from overseas. I could tell straight away from his voice that something was wrong. He looked at me but it seemed to take forever for him to get the words out.

'It's your mother. Your dad has passed away.'

Even in the shock of that moment I was irritated by his use of the euphemism. Why not just say 'died'? But by the time I took the phone, my throat was so tight I couldn't speak. Not that it was necessary as Mum launched in, talking at a million miles an hour.

'It was pneumonia,' she said. 'The old man's friend, they used to call it. He didn't suffer. I thought he wasn't right before you left, but I didn't say anything. After all, what was the point? He's really been gone for a year, when you think about it, and Martin needed you there. But he wasn't right – he died three days after you left …'

'What? When did he die?'

'Three days after you left. Remember I said I wouldn't let you know if something happened. It's been difficult not to tell you and we've had to keep the whole thing quiet in case one of your friends rang you in Germany ...'

My mind was as frozen as the wind outside as I tried to calculate precisely how long ago he'd died. So while I'd been answering polite questions from Martin's relatives about my father's health, he was actually already dead. It was as though I'd been existing in some parallel universe.

'What about the funeral?'

'Oh, there's no funeral. He's already been cremated, but I didn't go. None of us did. Dreadful place, the crematorium, evil. I didn't want to tell you, but Tim said it's getting so long that if I didn't tell you he would.'

I was struggling to process the information.

'Why didn't you let me know sooner?'

'Remember? We talked about this before you left.'

She was right. But we hadn't exactly *talked* about it; she had simply announced in her most matter-of-fact tone that if something happened to Dad she wouldn't tell me until I got back. I was used to such comments from Mum. She always said something to that effect before I travelled, even years before when both my parents were fit and well. Other people's mothers might say, 'Make sure you phone straight away if you need anything.' My mother says, 'Just enjoy yourself and I won't bother you if anyone dies while you're away.'

'Do you want me to come home?'

'No, heavens, no. What for? I'm *fine*.'

Marzipan & Magnolias

She sounded over-amped, like someone on speed. When I hung up Martin asked me what I wanted to do.

'I want to be near the water,' I said.

The kids were already asleep, and Dörte stayed with them while we drove to the ferry wharf. The howl of the wind was so loud we didn't bother trying to talk. I looked out over the black ocean and wondered which direction Australia was from where I was standing. It was literally at the other end of the earth.

That night I felt elated that Dad was free of that place. The indignity had ended. Then the numbness set in. We continued our daily routine of going over to the house and sorting things into boxes but I had the sensation of being contained in a pressure cooker.

I kept telling myself that it was good news, a release for Dad, for all of us after a year of torment. Why did it matter that I hadn't known? Why did it matter that there was no funeral? At night I'd lie awake in bed and wonder that I felt nothing. Nothing except the incessant tingling in my legs. I wondered if that was what a DVT felt like. There'd been lots of press about people developing a deep vein thrombosis on long flights and dropping dead. But I didn't recall tingling being a sign. And surely I wouldn't have one in both legs. But every night there it was, tingling from toes to thighs. The days dragged on. Finally I told Martin I had to go home – it didn't matter that there was no point. I just had to go home.

Sydney was at the height of its summer humidity when we arrived.

Max and Amy had taken the news better than I anticipated. They had found it so distressing to see his deterioration in the nursing home, perhaps to them it was a relief. Still, they were shaken; life didn't seem as secure as it once had.

Mum came over in the afternoon for a cup of tea. It was an awkward moment. We embraced somewhat stiffly but I could tell she was relieved to see me. I wondered how she had filled the past few weeks. It occurred to me that after a death, the bereaved busy themselves with funeral arrangements. But Mum had been busying herself with *not* making funeral arrangements. In fact, she'd been flat out keeping it all quiet, making absolutely sure there would be no fuss. She looked exhausted from the effort. I knew she had acted from the highest motives, but I felt so distant from her. The kids seemed to understand better than I did, how sad she must be. They sat with her and she asked them about their trip.

After she left I began sorting through the enormous pile of mail that had accumulated while we were away – mainly Christmas cards and bills. There were no letters from friends acknowledging Dad's death because no one knew. I wondered what Dad would have thought about that – even dying wasn't important enough to create a stir. You could just slip away, barely noticed.

Inadvertently, I opened a card addressed to Amy. It was from Beata, her piano teacher.

Dear Amy

I am sad to tell you that I can no longer teach you. There have been many changes in my life and I have to say good-bye. I am very sorry.

*I wish you all the best with your piano playing in the future.
With love from Beata.*

At the bottom, she had included the name of another piano teacher and his contact phone number.

There was something chilling about the note. I tried to call her, but the answering machine was on and I left a message. She did not return my call.

Over the next few days I became obsessed with finding her. I walked to her house as she lived near us, but she wasn't there. The tingling in my legs became almost intolerable with the exercise so, returning home, I lay down and waited for it to subside. An acquaintance, who Beata also taught, told me she had received a similar note. She believed Beata needed to leave Sydney to get away from her husband; that she wanted to start again.

I couldn't stop thinking about what must have happened in her life; I couldn't bear to think about another loss for Amy. That half-hour weekly lesson had been precious. No one else would be like her.

Still, I thought I should ring the new piano teacher, also Czech. His wife answered the phone.

'Yes my husband is not just piano teacher. He is performer. He is president of Classical Music Society here.'

As she rattled off her husband's credentials my throat grew tight and I felt the tears behind my eyes. My mind filled with pictures of Amy jumping around on the floor with Beata being the notes, her hugs and enthusiasm.

'What day would suit your daughter?'

'Tuesday. We used to go to Beata on a Tuesday.'

'Tuesday I can give you 4.45. Is that suitable?'
I didn't want to commit myself.
'My daughter has had trouble learning to read music.'
'My husband will be able to fix that. He is very efficient.'
'I just want her to enjoy it.'
'Yes, well, we'll see you on Tuesday.'
I hung up. I felt very empty.

My brother, Tim, arrived from Boston a few days later to stay with us. At night we sat together and he'd talk about Dad. He was still extremely upset by his death and wept unselfconsciously for minutes at a time. I watched him through my numbness, wondering where all this emotion came from.

I called in to see Mum every day, or she would come over for dinner. She kept saying it was a blessing that Dad was gone, that you wouldn't wish that sort of existence on a dog. It was all true, but I couldn't feel it. I couldn't feel anything.

One evening after dropping Mum home after dinner, I drove passed Beata's house. There was a light on in the living room. It was about nine o'clock – too late to drop in, but on impulse I parked the car, climbed the front steps and knocked. As I waited, it occurred to me that I was out of line. I really knew nothing about her circumstances or what could lead her to make such a dramatic decision.

She took a long time to come to the door, but finally she opened it. Her face was drawn and tired. For a moment we just looked at each other.

'What's happened?' I asked.

Her eyes filled with tears and she turned into the room leaving the door open and sat heavily on a sofa. I followed and sat beside her.

'I have to go,' she said.

The room seemed smaller than usual. There was a harsh fluorescent light that brought out odd colours I'd never noticed before. It felt artificial, like a studio set.

'Libby, I have to get away from here. This is not a marriage. I can start again.'

She looked at her hands, at her strong fingers.

'You know, I never wanted to study music but I had no choice. Both my parents were musicians. My mother taught me piano and she used to hit my hand with a ruler for each wrong note. Every Friday night I had to watch them perform even when I was too tired. They insisted that I study music at university.' She sighed. 'I always wanted to be a nurse or a doctor.'

I could see that her mind was made up. I felt very sad.

'How is Amy?' she asked.

'She doesn't know yet – I haven't told her.' We sat in silence for a moment. Then I said, 'My father died while we were away.'

'Oh, Libby, I'm so sorry.'

I started to cry. So did Beata. We sat there together on her sofa in that harsh fluorescent light and cried and cried for what we'd both lost.

It took four months to persuade Mum to come with me to the crematorium to collect Dad's ashes. In the end she agreed, but only after receiving a letter from the crematorium notifying her that they would only hold Dad's ashes without charge for six months from the date of cremation. After that she would have to pay a modest annual fee. Mum was outraged.

'The hide of them!' she kept saying.

'Mum, I'm happy to do it. You don't even have to be there.'

Although Mum didn't want to go, she wouldn't allow me to go without her. Predictably, it was almost impossible to pin her down to a date (bridge, gardening club, neighbor calling in for tea), but eventually we settled on a Wednesday morning in early autumn.

The car trip was strained, with conversations at cross-purposes.

'I know why you're upset,' she said. 'You've lost a parent.'

It was such an obvious statement, I didn't bother to respond. She continued.

'I was upset when I lost my mother and we weren't even close! Anyway, your father would regard driving all the way to the crem' as a ridiculous waste of petrol. It's an evil place. You know it's been bought by foreigners now, don't you?'

'I think it serves a purpose,' I said. 'It helps the grieving process.'

But she was having none of that psychobabble and called upon the wisdom of Great Aunt Alice to prove her point.

'Aunt Alice used to say that if you have a funeral everyone comes along and thinks they've done their bit. Aunt Alice didn't go to Uncle Frank's funeral, and she was still receiving invitations to lunch three months later.'

I knew that Mum missed Dad enormously, and this had not simply been a cynical exercise to obtain luncheon invitations, but it provided her with more evidence that she'd done the right thing. After parking the car, we sat together in silence for a few moments before going in.

At reception we were greeted by an obsequious man with stooped shoulders, wearing a dark suit. He took my mother's hand and introduced himself as Kelvin. Mum almost visibly recoiled from his touch. Kelvin's manner dripped with faux sympathy as I explained the purpose of our visit. He looked mildly startled when he learned that my father's ashes had gone unclaimed for four months. And the veneer briefly dropped again when my mother interjected that the only reason we were there at all was because the crematorium was going to charge us to keep my father there. But Kelvin recovered himself and ushered us into a tiny room, which for some reason was octagonal. Contained within each wall was a recessed shelf, displaying a different urn, each backlit for effect.

The man indicated for us to sit down as he took his place behind a small desk. From here he could point to the various urn options in which we could keep and even display our loved one from a prominent position in the house. He highlighted decorative features and alluded to price differences. It was then that Mum got the giggles.

At first I thought she must have suppressed a sob. But no, she was giggling. In that moment, I so badly wanted to join her. I looked at Kelvin, whose eyes darted between my mother and me. His veneer now all but gone, he soldiered on, choosing to fix his gaze on me as I still had some measure of control. Eventually I asked for the simplest and least expensive option. Delighted to be able to escape, he told us to wait and he'd bring our loved one to us.

Dad was presented to us in a surprisingly heavy Napisan-sized plastic tub, for which there was no charge.

Finally, on a sunny April morning, my brothers and I gathered under the pear tree at my parents' home for a send-off of sorts. Mum stayed inside, but she had bought a garden seat as a kind of memorial, which was positioned under the tree. I'd mounted a brass plaque on the seat back. It was engraved with the first verse of the A.A. Milne poem, 'The Four Friends', which Dad used to read us as children. Now the four siblings stood together, awkwardly at first, with Mark holding the heavy tub containing the ashes. He opened it and we all peered in. The course-grained contents were a far cry from the ethereal fairy dust I was expecting. We all took a moment to quietly absorb this unromantic fact. It was then clear we had no idea what to do next. What was the protocol for scattering a loved one's ashes?

Mark broke the silence by recalling some of Dad's best Mrs McGillicutty impressions. Around and around the pear tree he walked, jaw clenched in the familiar locked expression Dad assumed when reminded of his most annoying client. As he walked he began to empty the strange-looking contents of the tub onto the garden. He then passed it to me, and so, adhering to family hierarchy, we took it in turns to scatter our father's ashes. We then sat down on the seat Mum had bought. Knowing how much Dad eschewed any standing on ceremony, Mark supplied an impromptu eulogy:

Marzipan & Magnolias

This seat sits upon
The ashes of John
Although he is gone
His memory lives on.

20. Downsizing

THE YEAR 2001 must have been a popular time for travel. We certainly had more than our fair share of overseas visitors – mostly Martin's relatives, all of whom had received open invitations from him to visit us *Downunder*. Unfortunately, they descended upon us over a concentrated three-month period.

I knew it was important for Martin to see family from home after the loss of his parents, and for the kids to see their cousins, but it was becoming impossible for me to maintain the momentum required to keep this B & B going. I went into survival mode – but survival from what? Surely putting on an extra load of washing and cooking for a few extra people wasn't that difficult? There seemed to be no way to express the depth of fatigue I was experiencing.

'I can't manage any more visitors. Please *stop* letting your relatives come,' I said one night as I dragged myself into bed.

'That's a bit mean spirited,' said Martin. 'I thought the distraction would be good for you – for all of us. Anyway, I don't understand why are you're so tired all the time. Why don't you go to another naturopath – or doctor or something? And what about your diet? Didn't you say you wanted to eat organic?'

I was stung by his rebuke.

After we had returned from Germany I'd seen the neurologist about the tingling in my legs. He ordered a course of steroids but it hadn't helped. He re-tested my reflexes, all of which were normal.

'But what about the tingling?' I said. 'It drives me crazy – and if I walk more than about twenty paces it gets worse.'

'Yes, well we can't measure that so it doesn't count as a deficit. You're doing very well considering you've probably had MS since you were about twenty-five.'

But I didn't feel as if I was doing well. He suggested I might be depressed. Had I considered a course of anti-depressants? I left his office feeling worse than when I'd arrived. I was beginning to doubt myself – perhaps there was an element of self-indulgence after all.

For my birthday in February Natasha invited me to lunch at a waterfront restaurant on Pittwater. My first reaction was to come up with an excuse. On one of my few days without visitors I'd have preferred to sit in a catatonic state – not pick up the phone or step foot out the front door. But that would have been ridiculous, so I accepted as graciously as I could.

Our table was on a deck overlooking a secluded bay. The water was still, the air was still and low hanging clouds encased us in humidity. In every direction the foreshore was met by steep embankments covered in dense scrub or trees. The heavy silence was broken occasionally by the whining cry of a crow. It was claustrophobic.

Once our drinks had arrived Natasha got straight to the point.

'I wanted to find out how you are. We hardly ever see you

or Martin. How are you – you know, as a couple? You've been through a hell of a time.'

Her question caught me off guard. The truth was I was so preoccupied with getting through each day I had no idea how we were as a couple – hadn't even thought about it.

'I don't know,' I said. 'Life's so busy we don't really get much time to talk.'

'You probably need to spend some time together on your own. No visitors, no kids!'

When I got home I kept thinking about Natasha's question. Conversations between Martin and me were now mostly limited to the day-to-day essentials. That New Year's Eve party where we had optimistically toasted to 'no more dramas' felt like a lifetime away. It was as though we were orbiting separate planets of the same solar system, our paths rarely intersecting.

We were meant to be going out for dinner that night for my birthday, but by the evening I'd run out of steam. There was no way I could go anywhere. I was angry and frustrated with myself. Martin suggested he pick up take-away so we could make it a bit festive with Max and Amy, and a video, something feel-good. Something with Tom Hanks.

After the kids were in bed we settled in to watch the movie, one we hadn't heard of called *The Green Mile*. The opening scenes didn't have that 'Tom Hanks' feel we were looking for and soon enough his character revealed his wife had a brain tumour. Martin switched it off and we both kept staring at the blank screen. I wanted to cry.

By September the stream of visitors had died away, but I was no better. At the end of most days I looked as though I wouldn't see the year out. My face was white and there were dark circles under my eyes. So I avoided the mirror.

I continued to downsize my life. My garden, which I'd gone some way to reclaiming since our return from America, was slipping out of my control again. Sometimes I'd force myself to have a blitz on the weeds, filling up boxes with oxalis or nut grass, but it would take me days to recover from the effort. I reduced my work hours. Still, I wasn't managing. Eventually I took leave from work altogether, telling myself it was a temporary arrangement. I had my eyes tested. Perhaps glasses would help me get a better handle on my day.

'Your eyes are considerably weaker than they should be for a woman of your age,' said the optometrist accusingly. 'Have you ever had chronic fatigue syndrome?'

'No,' I said, vaguely aware that I was withholding relevant information.

She gave me exercises for 'optic hygiene'. I was irritated by her reaction – so what if I needed reading glasses. Was that so *abnormal*?

The glasses didn't give me what I'd hoped for, but at least I didn't have as much trouble reading the phone book. I avoided invitations to meet friends for coffee or lunch, so the invitations became less frequent. I knew I was isolating myself, but I couldn't help it.

Since my return to Australia, the only writing I'd done was for magazines. I hadn't managed to get into the creative groove I'd had in the US. But now, sometimes I'd sit at the computer

Marzipan & Magnolias

and write short bits or random thoughts, or I might add to the strange story I'd started in Cape Cod about the nameless girl with the neurological condition.

21. The Magnolia

THE MOMENTUM THAT HAD DRIVEN MUM during Dad's illness had now dissipated. She'd endured her grief privately, quickly closing any gaps that might allow an unguarded emotion to escape. In her practical way, she began filling her life with bridge games, garden clubs and Probus outings. She was very busy. It was difficult to talk about Dad, except for Mum reiterating the relief that he was no longer suffering and how sensible a decision it had been not to have a funeral. I had to bite my tongue during these exchanges.

One day when I called in, she was sorting through the many watercolours he'd painted in his retirement. She had spread them out over the dining room table, loosely sorted into piles.

'Look at this one,' she said, handing me a postcard-sized ink and watercolour of a Cornish fishing village, viewed from the sea. Whisper-thin pen outlines of houses on rocky outcrops were shaded with just a hint of colour.

'It's beautiful,' I said.

We worked our way through the paintings and sketches and selected some to have framed.

Mum insisted on going to a particular art supply shop to have the framing done. Together we spent hours of indecision over frames and mats, intrigued by people who could hand a painting over the counter and say, 'Just frame it.' Ours had to be perfect. It had to do justice to the work it contained.

Dad had always loved going to this art supply shop, and although Mum rarely cried, there was often a catch in her voice as she recalled those outings with him.

The framing shop became a regular excursion for us. When it was time to collect the work Mum presented her credit card and insisted on paying for mine as well. This was a surprise as she had never been extravagant; in fact, like many of her generation, she still lived on a Great Depression budget. 'It's my pleasure,' she said, when I went to protest, and she put her hand up to indicate that argument would be futile.

On the way home she suggested that we call in to a nursery 'for a browse'. We came upon an exquisite magnolia: tall and elegant with champagne-coloured blooms covering its bare branches. Mum read the label. It was Magnolia Elizabeth – my own name. My old Magnificent seemed ordinary by comparison. 'That is a must-have,' said Mum. 'It's silk.' ('Must Haves' would be a chapter in her book.) We both reached for the price tag. It was almost $400. Well, that's that, I thought, and after admiring it once more, we walked on.

Later that day, Mum rang me and said, 'I've ordered the magnolia for you. It's being delivered tomorrow.'

'No, that's silly. It's much too expensive.'

'Sorry, it's too late,' she said. 'Anyway you don't have a magnolia in this garden.'

This unexpected largesse was now making me nervous. I was sure there must be something she wasn't telling me, and suddenly the magnolia became a bad omen. I didn't want to accept it. The next day, however, it arrived in all its glory, ostentatiously throwing off blooms the size of side plates. I didn't know where to put it. A prominent position was required to acknowledge the generosity of the gift. But I couldn't bear a constant reminder of her impending demise, which I had convinced myself this signified.

Of course, I was being ridiculous and a suitable spot was found for the magnolia outside the large family room windows. The flowers continued their spectacle for several weeks and then died off as new light green leaves emerged.

I still wasn't feeling well. My eyes were bothering me. They felt stiff somehow if I tried to look sideways, and I was so tired. One night, as Martin and I were getting ready to go to friends for dinner, my legs felt like lead weights. As I walked, the floor appeared to be moving past my feet too quickly, like scenery whizzing past a train window. At our friends' house, things got worse. I was unsteady on my feet and then realised I was going to throw up. In a blind panic I ran for the bathroom, skidding on the tiled floor in my leather-soled shoes, arms flailing in an effort to stay upright. I lurched through a door, but it was the wrong one, and I startled a sleeping child. When I found the bathroom, I fell onto my knees, head over the toilet bowl. There seemed to be no end to the convulsions my body was going through to expel the demon. Eventually, I somehow stumbled to the front door, and we left unceremoniously, with a bowl provided by our astonished hosts. By the time we got home, I could not walk without help.

I was sick throughout the night, but only in the morning was the full extent of the problem revealed. In daylight I was met by a frightening kaleidoscope, a wild collage, made up of fragments of my bedroom. Curtains that used to hang to the left now floated at a jaunty angle up near the ceiling. The cupboards rocked to and fro, like the horizon viewed from a rolling ship, and the door was so high you'd need a stepladder to reach it. Worse still, everything was in duplicate. I still could not lift my head from the pillow without vomiting. Martin called an ambulance.

As he was throwing a few things into an overnight bag for me I heard the siren coming down our street. Why did they have to do that? Why did they have to make such a fuss? Thank God the kids had stayed the night with Mum. Martin let the ambos in. They were cheery and relaxed.

'All right, love, can you sit up for us?'

As soon as I tried I started vomiting again.

'She's been like this all night,' said Martin. 'And there's something wrong with her eyes.' His voice was small and worried.

They put a drip into my arm to stop the vomiting. As they positioned themselves to roll me onto a sling I could just make out a giant, black ambulance boot landing on my pillow. I started to cry.

'You'll be okay,' one of them said gently. Then they hoisted me into the air. My eyes were closed but I could visualise our progress through the house to the front door, followed by a burst of harsh sunlight as we proceeded up the front path to the gate.

Tears rolled silently off my cheek and slid down the side of the plastic sling.

Lying on a trolley in the Accident and Emergency department, I began making imaginary deals with the devil. What would I give up to get my vision back? My right arm? Both legs? Bladder function?

The Emergency Department was packed to capacity. On the trolley adjacent to mine was a young man who was having more or less constant seizures. I looked across with my wonky eyes. From what I could piece together from my visual jigsaw, his arms and legs were flailing out in all directions. A nurse closed the curtain between us, but I could hear the crashing of his limbs against the metal sides of his trolley. I half expected to be hit through the curtain. Over the racket, his parents were explaining that he'd drowned in a kayaking accident and someone had managed to revive him, but this was the legacy. I lay very still with my eyes closed, wondering about that poor boy's future.

I was seen by a doctor and told I'd be admitted and assessed by a neurologist. Mum would have to be told, but I couldn't bring myself to think about it. So Martin was dispatched to break the news and check if she could mind the kids for a bit longer.

After spending thirty-six hours in A & E due to bed shortages, I was wheeled to a two-bed ward. It was difficult to get a clear sense of my new surroundings, but I detected a large, sunny window overlooking trees.

Perhaps my world was already diminishing, but all I wanted was to have a shower and wash my hair. I would be able to think clearly if I could just wash my hair. Before helping me to the bathroom, a nurse placed a gauze patch over one of my eyes, pirate style. The patch eliminated the doubleness of my new world. But even then, the uncovered eye didn't function properly. I had lost perception of distance and size, so in the mirror my reflection appeared to be both alarmingly close and far away at the same time – like looking into a shiny brass doorknob. The top of my head appeared to be miles away and I wondered how I would reach it to wash my hair. Guided by the nurse and holding onto several sturdy rails, I undressed and stepped into the shower recess.

If I sat on a chair, I could shower alone. Closing my eyes, I let hot water run over my face, and imagined that I was in my own shower at home, where I could still see everything perfectly in my mind's eye. The sheer pleasure of washing my hair for the first time in three days temporarily erased all other thoughts.

A neurologist came to see me and explained that many people improve after such an attack, but how much and how soon was hard to say. However, the fact that I'd had three episodes in less than a year suggested that it was time to consider starting the injections. I winced at the thought.

Later, a social worker who looked about fourteen came in.

'I just wanted to find out er ... how you are going with your er ... illness,' she said in a mousy squeak.

I felt inexplicably affronted by her question. 'Fine,' I said. There was a certain satisfaction in seeing her squirm. She shuffled from one foot to the other and thanked me for my time.

Even as I gloated at this small victory, I wondered what my

problem was. Maybe it was an ego thing – after all, I was the health professional; I should be the one asking the questions. I recalled the ward rounds we used to do on Ward 17 each morning – the frightened faces, all hoping for a reprieve from the doctor. I used to wonder if they fantasised that the wrong brain scan had been read – that it was some other poor schmuck that should be in their bed.

Young medical students queued up and politely requested to see the performance of my uncoordinated eyeballs. Still, I did not want to believe it. I couldn't shake the feeling that this was somehow my fault.

That evening Martin returned. He sat quietly beside me and held my hand. After a while he said, 'I just didn't know. Well, I knew, but I didn't really get it. I'm sorry.'

'I know. I didn't get it either.'

'I've been living too much in my own head. We'll get past this – you'll see. We'll find a way.'

By the next day, with my eye patch on, I could walk if there was someone helping me, but I couldn't seem to hold my head exactly in the middle. I didn't really have a sense of where the middle was. This disorientation was compounded by the fact that the building I was in was round. The corridor was a circle from which the wards fanned off, as if by centrifugal force. Trying to hold my head up straight as well as walk at a continuous angle reminded me of the entrance-way to Coney Island at Luna Park, where the floor used to rise and fall underfoot, and mirrors distorted your reflection.

As I was walking with Martin I was aware that someone was approaching. I waited for her to alter course so we wouldn't collide, but she didn't. Finally we all stopped, face to face.

I looked into the eyes of an old woman, eyes full of pain. It was only then that I recognised Mum. I felt embarrassed or guilty to be caught out like this. How could I have let this happen? I wanted to cry.

Martin had done his best to put a positive spin on the situation, but clearly, by the look on Mum's face, she was having none of it. I couldn't bear for her to see me looking so pathetic. We returned to my room and she pulled up a chair beside the bed, wearing a determinedly funereal expression.

'How long have you known?' she asked without looking at me. She was rummaging around in a large plastic bag.

'A few years,' I said. 'This is only temporary – I'll get better.'

She pulled a pair of knitting needles and some olive green wool out of the bag and started casting on stitches.

'What are you knitting?' I asked.

'I don't know yet,' she said.

The agitated click clack of the needles unnerved me.

'Mum, I couldn't stand it if you were just going to sit there and knit.'

I sent her out to buy me some nighties. I just wanted long t-shirts. Nothing fancy, nothing with frills and definitely no faggoting. I knew she would analyse and scrutinise the qualities of each nightie before purchasing anything, so it would take her most of the day. I didn't want her to come back because I had no idea how to reassure her, to take the pain away.

Marzipan & Magnolias

I was given intravenous steroids for five days to shrink the plaque that had lodged at the nerve junction that controls coordination of the eye muscles. The steroids made me feel strange and hyped up.

When I was not being jabbed with needles for blood samples or having my drip adjusted, I listened to the radio. It was only a few weeks since the September 11 attack on the World Trade Centre. Martin and I had stood transfixed in front of the television early on that September morning, staring at the footage of those planes slamming into the side of the buildings, people jumping to their deaths and the slow motion collapse of the Twin Towers. Over and over we watched the disaster unfold on the screen. And we kept watching, as if there might eventually be a different outcome.

The enormity of what happened had been almost impossible to grasp and had somehow fused in my mind with my own situation. I was a news junkie hospital patient – hour after hour, day after day, clutching a portable radio, my mind was filled with the uncomfortable history of east and west that now made the inevitability of what had happened so obvious.

When we were in New York, Windows on the World had been a favourite bar we'd taken our many visitors to at the top of the Twin Towers. Up there near the clouds we had truly felt like Masters of our Universe. When I thought now about looking down almost five hundred metres to the street below, I realised it was too high. I was ashamed of my own ignorance, my complacency and lack of curiosity. I felt such a fool as I fumbled with the radio dials, knowing that I had taken too much for granted. The world had changed forever, they kept announcing over the airwaves, and lying there in my hospital bed, I knew that they were right.

In the evening the kids would ring to say goodnight. Amy was missing me. She tried desperately to think of interesting things to say so she wouldn't have to hang up. She asked me if I would get better. Yes, I said, knowing how reckless a promise this was. When they came to visit I had chocolates for them. This bribe and the promise of watching *Seinfeld* on my hospital TV kept them entertained for a while. Max was contained and quiet. You'd never know what he was thinking. He also asked if I'd get better, and I gave him the same bold reply.

When they left I pondered my future and I made another deal with the devil. I could see with piercing clarity that all I wanted was to be able to look after my kids. I wouldn't care if I couldn't do anything else, but I wanted to be able to look after my kids.

The day finally arrived to go home. Martin helped me to the car. It was odd to be outside among people rushing to and fro doing everyday things. As they tactfully stepped around me, I wanted to shout out that just a week ago I could rush around like that too; that I was not really a hospital patient.

It only took ten minutes to cover the short distance to our home, and I stood holding onto the gate for a few moments before going inside. I could not believe how much my life had changed in a few days.

Californian poppies filled the front garden, but even with

my eye patch on, I couldn't bring them into focus. A blur of colours – yellows, creams and pinks – floated past me as I slowly made my way up the sandstone path. The image was beautiful, but unreal, like a Monet painting – tiny brush strokes hinting at the reality.

I wanted to sit down and Martin took me to the family room. The afternoon sun was streaming in the windows. Through those windows, tall and bursting with health,

I recognised Magnolia Elizabeth. A chill ran up my spine as it occurred to me that perhaps this magnolia was never the harbinger of Mum's demise, but rather my own. I sat down with my back to the window.

The next morning Martin was reluctant to leave me alone. I assured him I'd be fine by myself if he dropped the kids at school and picked them up. He had clients to see and I needed to rest. When I woke from an afternoon sleep, I could smell tuna mornay, my least favourite meal from childhood. I wondered if it were some kind of olfactory hallucination. I made my way out to the kitchen to find Mum cooking up her signature dish.

'What are you doing?' I asked.

'I just thought this would save Martin the trouble.'

'Mum, thanks, but I'm not helpless. I can organise dinner.'

'I just thought …'

But I wouldn't hear of it. Under normal circumstances, I'd be thrilled not to cook dinner, but I couldn't bear to think I was dependent on Mum.

Later Martin called to ask if I needed anything.

'Yes, could you pick up something for dinner?' I asked, with at least the good grace to feel foolish.

In those early weeks I was so weak I could only stay up for an hour at a time. My legs felt like two weighty sandbags that I dragged behind me. Martin had just started his own business and I was meant to answer the phone when he was out. The office phone was difficult to hear from the family room and when I tried to rush to answer it my legs would not respond. It was like one of those nightmares where you're trying to run from a wild animal and your legs won't move and the scream won't come out of your mouth.

Gradually I became more confident walking on my own and my vision began to improve. It was still double, but the images were moving closer together and were less wobbly. Even so, Mum was still nervous around me. One afternoon when she was dropping the kids home from school, she mentioned, almost as an aside, that she would host Christmas Day at her place.

'But, we're meant to be having it here,' I said.

'Well, obviously that's not possible. You'll end up back in hospital.'

I bristled. There was something unbearable about being seen as an invalid by my mother, something against the natural order of things. Standing there on my shaky legs, I couldn't imagine hosting Christmas for twenty people at our house in a matter of weeks, but I felt that my tenuous grip on independence would be determined by my response.

'Mum, we're having Christmas here. Everyone can bring something, but we're having it here.'

'Okay, okay. If that's what you want,' she held her hands up in a placatory manner, as if trying to calm a flighty animal.

The days turned into weeks and my strength continued to improve. I started to sneak glances at the magnolia. It was proud and strong. Just over a month after coming out of hospital I woke up to find I could see normally. I closed my eyes and opened them again several times to make sure.

Mum called in later that day and found me without my pirate patch on. I made us a cup of tea. We sat down beside the windows in the family room, from where I could observe Magnolia Elizabeth, her large green leaves waving in the gentle spring breeze.

22. The Casserole Committee

'KEEP LOOKING STRAIGHT AHEAD,' said the neurologist, shining a piercingly bright torch into the back of one of my eyes, then the other.

He leaned towards me, adjusting his position as he re-angled the torch to inspect every nook and cranny of my eye sockets. I tried to maintain my focus on the wall ahead of me, but I was dying to take another look at the mole on his left cheek, which, for the duration of my hospital stay, had remained stubbornly in duplicate. Now there was only one. I didn't need his fancy torch to know that my eyes were now in alignment.

'I'm pleased with your progress,' he said at last.

This didn't begin to describe my relief that I could walk and I could see. It took much longer, however, for my strength to recover. I wanted to be up and about when the kids came home from school, to give them afternoon tea and hear about their day. At first that's all I could manage. The rest of my time was spent moving between my bed and the sofa and then back to bed again. Martin continued to bring dinner home most evenings.

I began to venture out of the house. I went to occasional

school functions during the day but my legs wobbled so much I half expected them to concertina into the floor. Still, I refused to talk about it with anyone but my closest friends, and even with them, I played it down. I was terrified of being defined by this illness. I smiled and chatted about class sizes and homework and deftly came up with excuses not to volunteer for class mother or tuckshop duty. But such shirking made me feel inexplicably guilty. I would go home early and collapse in a heap on my bed.

Over the next ten months I continued to make substantial improvements. In fact some days I felt almost back to normal, which confirmed the belief that I had clung on to: that this was all just an aberration. I would get better.

We were heading into a scorching summer, which brought another bushfire season, this time of biblical proportions around the whole country. It also completely flattened me. I was entirely sapped of energy, and on some days was unable to even hang out the washing. This innocuous task became the yardstick against which I measured my progress. If I could not even manage one load of washing, it was officially a very bad day. For the first time I began to really fear that this was a long-term problem. The crushing fatigue of mind and body felt incompatible with leading any kind of normal life. When I raised it at the next appointment with the neurologist he was unconcerned. It was not measurable and therefore not really worth discussing. His view continued to be that I was doing very well. That somehow served to only made me feel worse.

By February I had retreated into the four walls of my house.

I was lonely and becoming more isolated as the horizons of my world contracted.

Lying on my bed one day I was leafing through the school newsletter. An urgent cry had gone out for helpers for various committees. Immediately I felt the familiar guilt that accompanied these requests and my mind conducted the two-way debate that I was now used to. Come on, I thought, I'm not working. I have the time to help if I plan ahead. But hang on, I have MS. That's a good excuse isn't it? Even saying it aloud to myself, it sounded phoney. I scanned the list. Tuckshop, Class Mother, Spring Fair Organiser, Casserole Committee.

The Casserole Committee provided meals to families in need due to illness or death or some other crisis. I toyed with the idea. Cooking had never been my thing – maybe something to do with tuna mornay phobia – but it seemed the least demanding of the jobs and part of me wanted to sign up to appease my Protestant work ethic.

The debate continued in my head. No, I had to be sensible. There were plenty of mothers who could turn out a casserole without blinking an eye. I didn't have to justify myself. Just say no.

There was a meeting at the school to welcome new parents. I could manage that, I thought. At the end of the meeting, without any warning, a book was passed around for us to sign. I had an immediate sense of foreboding.

'What's the book for?' I asked the woman beside me.

'The Casserole Committee,' she said. 'They have trouble getting enough people to sign up.'

I'd walked into a trap. Suddenly the idea seemed absurd. What would I do if I were called upon when I wasn't well? What had I been thinking? Everyone was signing the book. I could hardly pass it on without signing it, when I was sitting there apparently hale and hearty. The woman on my right signed it and passed it to me. I signed it. I passed it to the woman on my left, who gave it a perfunctory glance and just handed it on.

I couldn't believe it. She just handed it on! No apologetic look or aside to me that she lived in the country, or had only one functioning arm. This woman's brazen ability to silently say no filled me with admiration. I wanted to lean across her and grab the book back and cross out my name.

That night as Martin unpacked the frozen lasagne he'd picked up on the way home, I told him what I'd done. He raised one eyebrow.

'You're going to cook for the Casserole Committee?' he said, setting the microwave to 'defrost'. 'Maybe they should be cooking for us.'

During one of my afternoon rests, Venus popped into my mind. It was roughly twenty years since she'd absconded from the neurology ward of St Vincent's Hospital. Of course, I understood her better now, her refusal to accept her condition and her desire to intimidate health professionals barely out of school. But perhaps it was time for me to find a different path. I tried to imagine calling the convener of the casserole committee and telling her I'd made a mistake, that I shouldn't be on her committee, that I had MS. The scene pictured in my mind's eye quickly fragmented and I knew I wouldn't do it.

One morning, the arts program on ABC radio, featured a short story, in which the author recounted her wedding night. It was sad and funny and was told with a light touch. At the time, my own writing was developing a bit of momentum. Even on bad days, I could nearly always manage to sit at the computer and write for a short time. The patchwork scenes I was constructing were evolving into longer pieces. Suddenly, I was desperate to connect with other writers.

The NSW Writers' Centre offered courses in memoir and life writing so I signed up for a ten-week course of weekly classes. For all my reluctance to reveal my diagnosis, I was able to write about it. My only interest was the clarity of the storytelling, and as such, it wasn't really about me. After the course concluded, I joined a writing group with the other participants, and just like in New York, these meetings quickly became the most important date on my calendar. Writing was something I could manage even when it seemed that my body was working against me.

23. The Wedding Photo

LIKE MOST PEOPLE, I've always loved going through old family albums. Snatches of lives, a thought or a moment captured, cryptic explanations inked on the back of small sepia prints. After Dad died I spent even more time going through those early photos. Dad as a jackaroo in western New South Wales, Dad on his VJ sailing boat with a friend, Dad with his dogs. He'd had many dogs in his life and he remembered all of them – Ginger, Blue, Kip, Dover. Even when his mind was going, he still remembered all his dogs. We now had a dog, too, a border collie we'd acquired after our return to Australia. Mum would ask me to take him over and let him jump up onto the bed beside Dad. It was, by then, the only thing Dad would really respond to.

It had been painful to watch Mum bear witness to Dad's relentless decline. Painful and frustrating. And since then her grief had been compounded by the knowledge of my diagnosis. I told her she should feel free to talk to her friends about it if that would help, but she declined the offer.

'I couldn't stand to be constantly asked about it – to be always reminded …'

That felt like a slap in the face – after all, I was the one living with it. And, once again, a line of communication was blocked. Still, I knew exactly what she meant and I wanted to somehow make everything better.

Her seventieth birthday was coming up and I was determined to find the perfect gift. However, buying presents for Mum has always been fraught with difficulty. 'I don't need anything,' she'd always insist. When my brothers went ahead anyway and bought her a gift, she usually made a quiet comment to me about how she already had three, or that this particular brand was known to fall apart as soon as you looked at it. I sometimes felt too apprehensive to even try. But for her seventieth, I wanted to get it right.

A wedding photo would be just the thing. I had recently noticed that she did not have a framed photo of her wedding anywhere on display, so I decided to find a wedding photo, have it enlarged and place it in a beautiful silver frame. All the photo albums as well as the masses of loose photos dating back generations were kept in a deep drawer at the bottom of a chest in Mum's living room. I called in when she wasn't home. I sat on the floor, pulled out the bottom drawer and opened one of the albums.

As a child I had loved the wedding photos from my parents' generation. Virginal white brides with long veils and elegant bouquets, attended by a gaggle of matching bridesmaids in silk taffeta gowns and pearls. The groomsmen in tails and short back and sides posed proudly for the camera. They all looked so optimistic. I now flicked through the familiar pages, and realised for the first time that there was no wedding photo of my parents.

All their friends were represented and Mum and Dad featured in most of the wedding party shots, but their wedding was not there. I checked all the albums, and then laboriously searched through the loose photos in the drawer – but not a single shot of my parents' wedding. Later, I asked Mum about it.

'Oh, there are no photos from our wedding,' she said. 'The photographer didn't show up. Someone took a photo with Dad's camera, but the slide was lost years ago.'

'Surely it's somewhere,' I said.

'No, I last saw it maybe twenty years ago. It's gone.'

My family has always been particularly bad at marking occasions, so I shouldn't have been surprised, but I felt somehow cheated that a piece of our history was missing. Even more unbelievable was that I'd never noticed. I wondered briefly if they had been forced to marry because of an unplanned pregnancy, but my mother roared with laughter at the suggestion. No, apparently nothing as glamorous as that – it was simply lost.

At least I now knew that it was a slide I was looking for. There were also boxes of slides in the drawer. I checked them, holding each one up to the light. Most I had never seen before, so I lingered over many shots, delighting in early pictures of my parents as young lovers – at a picnic or a railway station or on a drive in the country. But the one I was looking for wasn't there.

Someone must have had a record of my parents' wedding. I rang her closest friend, but she had not been at the wedding, nor did she have a photo. None of their friends had attended, she told me. It had been strictly a family affair.

Given that there was no scandal to hide, I wondered why it

had been strictly a family affair. Why did I know so little about it? Once again I tried to find out.

'My parents couldn't afford a wedding,' Mum said bluntly.

'But Dad's parents could.'

'Oh, I suppose it was a pride thing. The bride's parents were meant to pay.'

I felt deflated. When Mum wasn't home I went over and searched the spots in her rambling, disorganised house where old slides might have been stashed. Up in the roof in old Globite suitcases, in boxes in the garage, on the barely accessible top shelf of her wardrobe. However, after weeks of clandestine searching I had to concede defeat.

Her birthday was drawing closer. I'd have to choose a different picture to frame. There was a three-inch black and white of Dad with my older brother and me aged about six and two, which I knew she loved. I could see why. Dad looked tall and handsome, a young man going places. The newly planted garden in the background was brimming with promise of a successful future. Although financial success always eluded Dad, nothing could erase the optimism of this early photo.

Sometimes I wonder what sort of person he would have been if his working life had been different. Perhaps a political cartoonist instead of a real estate agent flogging houses to support too many children. When he was in the nursing home, small and confused, he still occasionally sparkled with his satirical humour. One day I asked him if he would choose to have four children if he had his time over again. Although he no longer remembered how many children he had, he looked thoughtful and then with a wry smile said, 'I think I'd start with one and see how it went.'

I looked back at the photo. I'd have it enlarged and find the ideal silver frame. It would have to be entirely plain, and perfectly proportioned. This seemed like a straightforward task, but every square frame I found had some form of decoration – little bows or swirls – embossed onto the silver, something that I knew Mum would hate. If it were not perfect, there'd be no point buying it at all. She'd hate the thought of all that wasted money.

When I had almost given up, I came across a beautiful, completely plain silver frame in the right size for the enlarged picture. With the photo inside, it made a beautiful gift, but for me it was still a poor second to the wedding photo.

My birthday falls the day after Mum's, so we usually have a joint celebration. This year she arrived at my house early with one of my brothers as Amy and I were setting the table. We had a glass of wine while we waited for the others to arrive. When we were all assembled the gift was presented. I was stupidly nervous. I'd know from her voice if it hadn't worked. It seemed to take forever for her to read the card and unwrap it.

She was quiet. She held the frame, running her fingers around the smooth edge, and looked at it for a long time. 'What a beautiful frame,' she said at last. Then with a catch in her voice, 'That's my favourite photo of Dad.' I could hear from her tone that it was right. Then she said, 'I have a present for you, too.' This was unusual. Mum had never had a present for me on (or even close to) the actual day.

She handed me a small parcel, bundled loosely in white tissue paper. I peeled off the paper, which revealed a photo I had never seen before in a simple, silver frame. A young couple, the woman in an elegant grey-blue gown and the man in a dark suit, were standing together on the front steps of an old sandstone church, probably in the 1950s. It took a moment for me to realise that it was the lost wedding photo.

I was looking at my parents as they were on that December day forty-eight years ago. Dad looked so young and proud in his smart suit with a gardenia at his lapel. He'd had his hair cut for the occasion. Mum looked stunning. Her dress was in deep pewter blue lace over yards of matching taffeta. Mum has never been conventional, but for the 1950s, a blue bride must have been particularly unusual, and of course, she would never have considered anything as fussy as a veil. A wide V-neckline framed a double string of pearls at her throat. Her left hand had been released from the elbow-length gloves in the same blue, to allow for the placement of the wedding ring, and she held a small posy of flowers in that hand. The other arm was looped through Dad's. I couldn't stop looking at the photo.

'Where did you find it?' I asked at last.

'At the bottom of a box of slides of Mark as a newborn baby,' she said. She looked so pleased. 'The same roll of film must have been in the camera when he was born. I'd never thought to check in there.'

For days I couldn't stop looking at the wedding photo. It was like peering through a window directly into my parents' past. How I wanted to be able to talk to this handsome couple about their hopes and plans for the future. They seemed to gaze back at me across the years, glowing with youthful naïveté, and I found myself feeling oddly protective of them.

24. French Polish

WHEN I WAKE UP EACH MORNING, I check to see if it's there: the monkey that I carry around most days of the week. Sometimes it's a little spider monkey that I barely notice; other times it's a big baboon. On baboon days, it takes great effort to achieve even the simplest things. For me, that's what living with multiple sclerosis is all about – the size of the monkey.

Some mornings I start out monkey-free – strong and ready to take on the world. As I organise breakfast and school lunches, the radio plays in the background. There are continued reports on the plight of children held in detention and more suicide bombings in Iraq, the announcer's mild voice in such stark contrast to the magnitude of the human tragedy. Politicians dodge and obfuscate, treating the general public like the apathetic lot we are. Driving the children to school, I think about becoming an activist. Perhaps I could visit detainees at Villawood. The very least I could do is bombard politicians and newspapers with letters.

I can already tell today's monkey will be a challenge. It's getting hot when I arrive home, and my limbs are starting to feel spongy from the heat, as though my joints are now made of rubber. I turn on the air conditioning to try to reverse the effect. It's already clear this will not be one of my better days so I'd better get started on those letters before I run out of energy. Before that, though, I have to do my daily injection, which began after the 'eye episode'. I hate giving myself these injections but supposedly they reduce the number and severity of attacks by thirty per cent. The truth is, though, it's a numbers game. It's about averages of large groups of patients, not about me. There's no way of knowing whether it will work on me, or how well or for how long it will work on me. For now, though, things have stabilised so I'm going with the numbers.

By the time I switch on the computer, my legs have progressed from spongy to heavy, but I try to ignore it. The study is on the northeast corner of the house with windows overlooking my favourite part of the garden. Viewed from this vantage point, it is a luscious collage of greenery, with a tempting garden seat at its heart. Now, thanks to the manpower of a proper gardener, it is becoming what I envisaged for it years earlier. There is something nourishing about this vista and I usually feel at my most productive sitting here at my desk.

On the screen the cursor blinks at me, and despite the weightiness of my limbs, I'm filled with an urge to write expansively. I start out well enough, peppering the text with a string of dis-words: disenfranchised, disaffected, disappointed, but after a few paragraphs, my concentration falters. Gradually, inexorably, the world closes in around me and I give up. This is the worst part, and the hardest to describe. It's as though a big set of horse blinkers has been applied to my head, narrowing my field of vision, preventing me, both figuratively and literally, from seeing the big picture. The strange thing is that my vision is completely normal, so it's more of a perception than an actuality, but I am at a loss to overcome it. A familiar sense of frustration wells up in my chest. There seem to have been a lot of days like this lately and I'm worried that something is brewing, that I might be heading for another nasty episode. As scary as that thought is, in irrational moments I find myself almost willing it on, as though it would clear the air, earning me some kind of reprieve that would allow me to move forward again.

I save the paltry twenty-five word document and leave the study. If I hang out a load of washing, at least I'll have achieved something, according to my yardstick. In the laundry I wrestle with the bed sheets that have wound themselves tightly around the blades. Tugging and wrenching, I half expect them to tear in two. How is it possible they could they be so firmly stuck? Finally, with the basket full, I open the laundry door and find myself engulfed by humidity. The air is heavy, and walking to the clothesline is like wading through thick soup. One by one I hoist the wet sheets up onto the line. It's a marathon effort as I raise all those kilopascals of air pressure above my head with them. The sheets hang limply in the sticky air.

Returning to the house, I go straight to my room and flop onto the bed. As my body and brain shut down, a small window remains open somewhere. Thoughts bump into each other, forming themselves into words, then pithy sentences for the letter I was working on. I want to write them down so I don't forget but I can't. My arms are like lead weights and choose not to respond. Soon my mind is also numb. No more thoughts of refugees or politicians. Just before I fall asleep, images of Dad come into focus. Dad as he was in the nursing home, lying flat on his back, eyes closed, cheeks sunken. Towards the end, those waking moments when his personality still shone through were rare. Sometimes I'd have to check if he was still breathing. Dad died of tiredness. Well, his diagnosis was vascular dementia, but to the layperson, he died of tiredness. He simply got too tired to eat or drink or even care that he was slipping away.

The sharp ringing of the telephone shocks me into consciousness. I practise saying 'hello' a few times before answering so I don't sound as if I've been asleep.

'Hello?'

'Hi Lib ...were you asleep?'

'No, of course not. How are you, Tash?'

It's Natasha. Busy Natasha, who now runs her own business, has three active children and never needs to have a rest during the day.

'We're organising a picnic for Sunday,' she says. 'We'll park near the zoo then walk to Middle Head. I think it's going to be hot, though. Would you be interested?'

This reference to the heat is her acknowledgement that it might be difficult for me. Still, I'm reluctant to admit it. The truth is that I'd rather die than lug a picnic basket along Middle Head Road in this weather. Maybe I *would* die – I'd just melt into the pavement, reduced to a puddle. Of course, I don't say that. Instead I say that I think we have something else on.

Why do I avoid the issue like that? Why do I continue to

pretend I lead a normal life? And with Natasha, of all people. It has something to do with my own fatigue prejudice. It feels like a cop-out. Or maybe it feels like I'm turning into Dad in the nursing home. Either way, I know it's silly and I resolve to call Natasha back later and fess up.

Most people with MS will tell you it's the humidity that's the killer, but I still remember a time that I loved it. Summer holidays at Evans Head where the temperature burned and the humidity soared. That never bothered me. I soaked up the sunshine at the beach or wandered barefoot through the scrub down to the river over hot, sandy soil, watching out for death adders and redbacks in my path. I remember the sweltering air, my sticky, salty skin and the pungent smell of horsehair mattresses and mosquito coils. There was something intoxicating, even dangerous, about the sensual atmosphere. From the verandah, I'd gaze up at the high blue sky; the world was expansive and energising.

These days, from the safety of mid-winter, I might catch myself yearning for the feel of that dense air against my skin. Or in the springtime, the sound of an out of season blowfly might momentarily fill me with a sense of anticipation: the summer is almost here. It only lasts a moment, of course, and I remember that the humidity is my enemy. It's an odd sort of loss that I feel; those extended summers still exist, but I am no longer a participant. Now my obsession is waiting for signs of a cool change.

Some years autumn arrives right on schedule. Other years the summer clings on for all its worth. This is one of those years. The days are closed in with cloud, not thick enough to keep out the heat, but enough to amplify its intensity. It's almost April and

I'm beginning to take it personally as each day passes without relief. My arms and legs tingle with pins and needles and I've been wondering if a new plaque has lodged in my spine. The neurologist isn't worried. I love that. Of course *he* isn't worried, but I am. When I saw him recently, he told me to call him if the symptoms worsened. I can't say for sure if they are worse or not. I called yesterday but he is away at a conference. His receptionist told me to go to Emergency if I was concerned. I don't think my symptoms warrant that and I couldn't face it anyway. This is the MS roller coaster-guessing game of chicken we play.

I force myself back to the study to finish the letter. On paper, at least, it sounds as if I'm bursting with energy, and with a very small degree of satisfaction I send off this one letter to a newspaper. So much for the barrage I was planning. No more time today because I have to get to the shops to pick up some essentials before the kids get home.

Today as I walk through the centre I almost collide with a woman who is rushing towards the nail parlour. It's a curious thing that nail parlours have sprung up all over the city, but have not even registered a blip on my radar. I wonder what the attraction could be. I peer in through the shop window. The glass is frosted up to shoulder height, so I almost have to stand on tiptoe to see properly. I feel voyeuristic as I watch the clients inside. Who are they and why are they here? On one side is a row of padded dentist-type chairs with a footstool at the base so clients can recline in comfort as their toenails are attended to. On the other side are small tables with a desk lamp and a tray of equipment. There is not one vacant spot. The manicurists (or are they nail artists? nail therapists?), wearing industrial face masks to protect them from chemical fumes, sit bent forward in concentration over their clients' hands; two women in such close proximity. One client is talking on a mobile phone, trapping it precariously between her chin and shoulder, another is watching intently, perhaps ready to pounce if the work is not up to standard, but mostly they just sit. A consultation finishes and the customer pays at the counter, treating her nails somewhat gingerly as she manipulates a credit card from its tight slot in her wallet. She leaves, quickly melting into the crowd. I wonder where she is going, what she plans to do now with her new nails.

How did this become so ubiquitous without my noticing? I imagine the advertising slogan: 'Come into my parlour for beautiful nails that tell the world who you are.' A French polish (or is that for furniture?) or even better – an artificial French polish glued to your existing nails. Come back every three weeks to maintain this new you. But what happens if you don't? The layers peel away and it's just you with your work-a-day nails.

The shopping centre has two nail parlours and countless hair salons, full of foil-covered heads and hair dryers blowing new styles and images into people's lives. Women's lives. It's a shopping centre full of women. Suddenly, I want to reach out to all these women, to show solidarity, maybe even compare monkeys.

Despite the endless musings that shopping centres offer, I have to stay focused or I'll run out of steam and end up going home empty-handed. I look at my list: bananas, Whiskas, toothpaste, dinner. The last item on this pathetic list is the tough one: dinner. My mind goes blank at the thought. I walk past all the trays of red meat. Yuk. How about chicken? Not again. I'll just buy a pie. Expensive, I know, but I tell myself I won't do it again. Tomorrow I'll develop a meal plan. Not even a small part of me believes this resolution, but it salves my conscience enough to go ahead with the purchase.

At the checkout I look at the other people in the queue, some with French polish, some without. Some with a huge trolley full – that must be their weekly shop. That's what I should do instead of calling in all the time for bits and pieces. My trolley looks as if I live alone with my cat. I wouldn't even consider going home without dinner for the cat – a successor to Winston but lacking his empathy. When I pull into the driveway, she's already waiting for me, mewing her list of grievances. She doesn't care that I don't feel great. The dog, on the other hand, tries to co-operate by eating tinned food, but it makes his stomach play up, resulting in unscheduled episodes on the carpet, so there's no choice but to provide him with boiled chicken. Sometimes, when the kids get home they ask what's for dinner.

'Nothing,' I say.

'So, what's that on the stove?'

'That's for the dog. You can have whatever's left over.'

The kids know about my MS and don't seem to find it strange that the animals' meals take priority over theirs. Somehow, even on a bad day, they know that a meal will end up on the table – even if it's brought home by Martin. However, this week he is away, so it's down to me.

Over dinner, which tonight is the alleged last-ever store-bought pie, I hear about their day; the highs and lows of being a kid, a teenager, a girl, a boy. Max wonders aloud whether it's better to drop your girlfriend of two weeks standing before she drops you. Despite my overwhelming urge to rest my head on the table, I put in my ten cents worth about compassion, but for him it's more about pride. Suddenly, Amy lets out a wail as she remembers a science assignment is due the next day. Her bottom lip trembles at the thought, but offers of an explanatory note to the teacher are rejected, as she confesses that the assignment is already late. Silently, my mind contorts into a version of *The Scream*. At this point I have no interest in analysing the rights or wrongs of rescuing my daughter from a fate of her own making. If we don't cobble something together from the Internet on the life cycle of frogs, none of us will get any sleep tonight. My nerves are further frayed during the usual after dinner argy-bargy over whose turn it is to clear the table, load the dishwasher and take out the garbage until I can't stand it anymore and banish them both from the kitchen. Suddenly I don't care if it's still a mess in the morning. I just want to get the life cycle of frogs written and go to bed. It's this last half hour that requires the greatest effort on my part not to lose the plot.

Finally, as I'm kissing Amy goodnight, she says, 'You're so lucky, Mum. You don't have to go to school or do homework. You can just do whatever you like.' I don't bother to point out who did tonight's homework. As I try to extract myself from her vice-like grip around my neck, she starts her impersonation of TV characters that she knows will make me laugh, no matter how tired I am. This buys her another five minutes, but eventually she has to concede that it's time to say goodnight.

I brush my teeth and quietly withdraw into my bedroom. Another day can be ticked off the summer calendar – surely the cool change will be here soon. I love the solitude of this corner of my house, where my mind can slow down like a whirring propeller gradually coming to a halt. I've done nothing about the war in Iraq, nor have I lobbied my local member about refugees, or even reached out to my monkey-carrying compatriots at the local shopping centre. But I have hung out a large load of washing, written one letter, rescued my daughter from the wrath of her teacher, and given my son relationship advice. Not bad, considering the weight of today's monkey.

Researchers seem confident that one day there will be a cure for MS, but in the meantime, glancing down at my nails, I wonder whether it would help if I had the occasional French polish.

25. Sounds and Silence

AT LAST AUTUMN ARRIVES WITH ITS brilliant crisp air and splash of colours, and months of sticky grime dissolves. There is something about it that fills me with optimism and a sense of – what?

That this order to the seasons is perhaps even more than it seems. Of course, coming from a long line of atheists I know that can't be right.

When I was a child, Mum sent me to Sunday school (we were Protestant-atheists and it was the 'done thing'). There I was taught that if you believed in God, miracles could happen. I took this important news home, but the message from my parents was clear: it was all a load of rubbish. Worse than rubbish; religions were evil things run by evil people, responsible for most of the wars of history.

Once I outgrew Sunday school my main exposure to religion was through our next-door neighbours, Stella and Pat and their two daughters, who were Roman Catholic. The girls attended schools with extravagant names, like Sacred Heart or Blessed Little Sisters of the Lamb or something. They went to confession (a fascinating concept) and I would wait to hear how many Hail Marys or Our Fathers were required of them for the sins of that week.

My parents scoffed at such nonsense as being almost as primitive as witch doctors in Africa, but this system of retribution appealed to my unsophisticated notion of justice. More than that, though, I wanted to know what it felt like to be on the inside, to be able to chant the lines that pass rhythmically back and forth between priest and congregation. I wanted to be a member of the club.

Stella seemed to attend a lot of funerals. Almost weekly, she'd be off to yet another wake in her Sunday best, carrying a plate of sandwiches. But to my parents, the fuss and expense of funerals were just further evidence of the exploitative nature of religion.

So even after the loss of two grandparents and one beloved elderly neighbour, I had never been to a funeral. My curiosity with this after-death ceremony grew, as I wondered what went on there, and why my brothers and I were not allowed to attend. Perhaps that's why we used to hold a service if we found a dead bird or mouse in the garden and we'd mark the site with a cross, made from twigs and string.

When I was twelve, Mum reluctantly allowed me to go to a Crusader Camp organised by the school. This was far more serious than Sunday School as I now learned that our souls were in mortal danger if we did not embrace the teachings of Christ. But no amount of reasoning could persuade my family. They rolled their eyes when I tried to say Grace before the meal and my brothers told me to shut-up so they could hear the television. In fact, any talk of religion was met with an impatient sigh, and another reminder of its wicked history.

Although my school was officially Anglican, chapel services were less theatrical than their Catholic equivalents. Our chaplain was an affable fellow, with realistically low expectations of his students' religious commitment, so his services were moderate in their delivery. However, sometimes there might be an occasion for a visiting clergyman to speak to us, perhaps someone used to a more devout congregation, and the sermons became weighed down with references to good and evil, and warnings of the consequences of straying from the teachings.

Despite the allure such rigid guidelines had held for me when I was younger, these threats now began to ring hollow. I was finding it increasingly difficult to understand how True Believers make that essential leap of faith, and I wondered if it were too late for me, having not received the relevant programming at an early age. In any case, the whole thing just didn't add up. I looked at the girls at school who announced their Christianity by wearing a small silver fish on their collar, with a mixture of curiosity and skepticism.

Although my parents were against all religions, I knew Mum thought Catholics posed a greater danger than Protestants, after all, they had the weight of numbers on their side by having so many children. But how could two religions, so similar in their theology, provoke such prejudice? To say nothing of Muslims, Hindus and Jews. 'Ratbags, the lot of them,' Dad would say. While each religion seemed to claim the moral high ground, backed up with historical evidence for their assertions, as far as I could tell, none of them had a credible story. They were exclusive clubs that I no longer had any inclination to join, and thoughts of spirituality receded to the back of my mind.

Sinead, my flatmate in London, was always lending me books, often with a Catholic bent that I found a bit wearing. One book, however, really captured my imagination. It was about a group of university students in London in the 1950s and '60s who tried to make Catholicism work for them even as they wrestled with moral dilemmas, such as artificial contraception and pre-marital sex. The book renewed my fascination with the complex layers of rules and rituals, the hierarchy of sins so intrinsically understood by the characters. Not that they didn't fight against it, but it is fair to say that religion was very much a part of their identity.

Sinead, brought up in Catholicism, believed whole-heartedly in God and the power of prayer. So powerful could it be that for important issues it was worthwhile to do a Novena, where a daily visit to the Church and extra candle lighting gave you a very good chance of having your prayer answered. Her father, for example, had done a Novena after her final exams, and she got 100 per cent in English. This really was the stuff of witch doctors.

I concluded once again that it was, in fact, a load of old rubbish. How could educated people in the late twentieth century not see what was patently obvious? Religions, all of them, were just mankind's pre-scientific attempts to make sense of the world around them, with the additional benefit of providing a form of social control (although, I conceded this did not explain the 100 per cent in Sinead's English paper).

Many years passed with no more thought on the subject until

Dad died. Although I was, by then, well versed in my family's ideology, I felt let down by it. To my surprise I craved the ritual of a church service, of flowers and people in black. I craved the opportunity to hear his friends talk about what a great bloke he had been.

About a year later, I went to the funeral of a friend's father. He had lived to a ripe old age and had not gone down without a fight. It was a grand occasion with lots of suits, hats and sunglasses. One daughter flew out from England, one came from Western Australia with husband and four children in tow. There were many people there whom I hadn't seen since university days and I felt as if I'd slipped into *The Big Chill*.

Eulogies were delivered by tearful daughters, respectful sons-in-law and wide-eyed grandchildren. The widow remained seated at the front of the church, dignified, in a lilac linen dress and sunglasses. A line was quoted that her husband had used at their fiftieth wedding anniversary: 'Darling,' he'd said, 'our marriage has been the longest stand-up fight in history, and I've loved every minute of it.' That's when I started to get a little misty. Then they played *Blue Moon*, which was apparently 'their song', and suddenly I couldn't stop the floods of tears that followed.

I thought about that funeral over the next few days. I wanted to thank the family for having it. I wanted to tell them that it was a bloody great funeral.

For a short while, I could have been tempted to become a funeral junkie. I realised this when a friend cancelled our lunch date because she had yet another funeral to go to (she'd married a Catholic), and I felt just a twinge of envy.

Elizabeth Lancaster

'I'm dreading it,' she said. 'I hate funerals. Your mother had the right idea, you know.'

Indeed, shaking off my parents' strident views on the topic is not a simple matter. After all, it's true that religions are responsible for many of the wars of history, and maybe there are too many shallow men in black suits. But I've finally realised that's not the point. I wonder if religion hasn't given spirituality a bad name. Certainly, my parents would not have discerned a difference between the two.

Recently we stayed with Peter, the eccentric artist Martin lived with when he first came to Sydney on his backpacking holiday. Peter's studio is on his family's sheep property in the Southern Tablelands. Martin and I have spent a lot of time there with the children over the years, and we still visit when we can.

Peter's place is a meeting point for artists from all over the world. He hosts exhibitions, charity concerts and fund-raising balls in his corrugated iron concert hall. It is simultaneously a place of great energy and serenity; a place where you feel that anything is possible. One night, very late, I woke to the strains of classical music. I knew it must be Peter playing the grand piano in the concert hall, now empty. The music travelled unhindered across the paddocks on the night air. Through the curtainless window beside my bed, I gazed into the vast black sky and imagined the Milky Way gliding past us overhead.

My thoughts wandered back to school days, and how much I had loved singing the hymns. It wasn't their content, but rather a sense of being part of something larger that was producing beautiful music. Five hundred voices filled the chapel, as together we became more than the sum of our parts.

I still love singing and music, and now I also love silence – like the silence of our old house, its timber floors, the plaster walls and the thick glass windowpanes that distort your view if you look from a certain angle. When we bought this house in its quiet street in a quiet suburb, I found the silence overwhelming, but I grew to understand it. More than that – I grew to depend on it. In the heat of summer, when my strength is tested to its outer limits, I retreat into my house. At first it was like a prison sentence, but now, when I'm alone here, I sit quietly, absorbing the stillness from the walls around me.

Sometimes from my back verandah I might see a bank of storm clouds or a crimson sunset or a flock of cockatoos, and I'm filled with that same strange, intangible sense that I had when singing the hymns at school: a sense that I'm playing my small part in something grand. I don't know if that feeling comes from within or without, and when I see my children racing each other through our front gate after school each day, I'm not sure that the distinction really matters.

It's autumn, just over three years since Dad died. Outside, the leaves are starting to turn; the snow pears, weeping mulberry and blue spruce are preparing for the winter. The rhythm of the seasons, like a complex piece of music, is full of sounds and silence in perfect balance. Mum sometimes says that whenever her time comes, she hopes it is not at the end of winter. It would be such a shame to miss the spring.

Afterword

Since *Marzipan and Magnolias* was first published, I have had many questions from readers about what happened next. Although I had reached a point understanding and acceptance of both my diagnosis and the relationship with my mother, the course my illness would take was unknown. I am relieved and a little surprised to report that I am doing extremely well. This is no doubt due to a combination of factors: an improvement in medical treatments, an increase in energy reserves as my children have grown up and left home, and dumb luck! I make no assumptions about the future, but enjoy what I have right now.

In this expanded edition, I have filled out some areas that I felt would benefit from further detail or explanation. There are also several minor changes, such as the name of the town where my mother grew up, which I had concealed for her privacy. She is from Kyogle in northern NSW, not the nearby town of Casino. Visits to Kyogle were an important part of my childhood and I wanted the name of this pretty town to appear in the text. Similarly, my grandfather's name was Chester, not Arthur, and lastly, my childhood dog's name was Puff, not Duffy (don't ask me why I needed to protect her privacy).

Currently I am completing my second memoir. If you would like to stay up to date with my writing and read other stories, please visit my website:

www.elizabethlancaster.com.au

Acknowledgements

Heartfelt thanks go to my writing group for their endless support and encouragement in this project: Emily Reed, Fay Redgrave, Nicole Bradshaw, Phyllis Gorman, Marion Nicolson, and especially to Meredith Melville-Jones who meticulously proofread and suggested changes right up until the end. Also many thanks are due to my friends Catriona Donagh and Vanessa Bednall for reading drafts and providing invaluable feedback. Finally, I would like to thank my husband and children for allowing me to mine our lives for material for this book.

About the Author

Elizabeth Lancaster began her working life as an occupational therapist in Sydney. In her mid-thirties, whilst living in the US with her husband and two young children, her life took several unexpected turns. On a whim and with a nudge from a friend, Elizabeth signed up for a writing course in New York. Fully immersing herself in it, she believed she was exactly where she was meant to be. Then she was diagnosed with multiple sclerosis. These two things have always been inextricably linked for Elizabeth. Writing became an essential part of accepting her new reality. On returning to Australia, Elizabeth wrote on a freelance basis for some years before turning her attention to memoir. Her humorous and engaging stories of family and relationships, set against larger events, explore universal themes.

Elizabeth lives in Sydney's north with her husband, comedic dog and family of canaries, all of whom continue to provide rich material. She is currently completing her second book.

Contact Elizabeth via her website at:
www.elizabethlancaster.com.au

Reviews

Elizabeth Lancaster has optimism, buoyancy and a sense of humour, as well as a strong appreciation of human foibles, including her own. This is an honest account of a difficult time, but told with a very light touch.

 - *Jacqueline Kent, author and member of the finch Memoir judging panel*

With sublime naturalness and an easy gift for telling her own story, Lancaster captures the unexceptional life of a middle-class Australian.

She grew up in Sydney, became an occupational therapist, worked at St Vincent's Hospital, met a German backpacker, lived and worked for a time in London, went to Germany and settled in, returned to Australia and got married, bought a house in the inner city and had two children.

All the while Lancaster's mother, a typical worrying Australian mum, was hovering in the background questioning the correctness of marrying a German, insisting on a church wedding and trying to do the right thing (which so frequently was the wrong thing) to ensure her daughter's happiness.

Anyone contemplating writing their memoir should use this as the benchmark. It is honest, fresh and written with a fine sense of balance.

- *Bruce Elder, Spectrum, Sydney Morning Herald, January 2011*

The title of this book intrigued me from the beginning. Marzipan and Magnolias...what a delicious invitation into first-time author Elizabeth Lancaster's life story. Winner of the 2010 inaugural Finch Memoir Prize (beating 75 other budding authors), *Marzipan and Magnolias* is a touching memoir of Lancaster's life, taking us across the seas as she connects with 'all things Irish' to battle multiple sclerosis while maintaining a determination to keep her diagnosis from her overbearing mother. As a young woman, Lancaster leaves Australia to escape her eccentric mother and follow her dreams. She finds love, but her subsequent marriage and relocation is barely acknowledged by her mother. Over the years, Lancaster and her young family visit Australia, and Lancaster hopes her mother will come to accept the decisions she's made. I thoroughly enjoyed this honest, sad at times, yet humorously told story. Lancaster's ongoing quest for independence, muddled with an almost overwhelming yearning for her emotionally detached mother's approval, is movingly conveyed. I would recommend this story to almost anyone – it's a real page-turner.

- *Sharon Athanasos, freelance reviewer and former bookseller.*
BOOKSELLER+PUBLISHER. September to November issue, 2010

www.ingramcontent.com/pod-product-compliance
Lightning Source LLC
Chambersburg PA
CBHW030528010526
44110CB00048B/782